Unhindered

T H I R T Y   D A Y S

Cover design by: Hannah Lockaby

ISBN: 978-1-954089-64-8   2 3 4 5 6 7 8 9 10 11

Printed in the United States of America

Charity Byers, Ph.D.
John Walker, Ph.D.

Unhindered

THIRTY DAYS

DISCOVER HEALING, FREEDOM, & POWER WITHIN

AVAIL

www.theunhinderedlife.org | @theunhindered.life

ACKNOWLEDGMENTS

Just as it often takes a village to "train up a child in the way he should go" (Proverbs 22:6, ESV), it took the collective gifts of *The Unhindered Life* team to give meaning and direction to this book. Being on mission together has been an immense privilege.

We are thankful for each member of *The Unhindered Life* creative team who brought their gifts, precision, and camaraderie to this project. Their contributions to vision, graphics, and editing have left a meaningful mark on this project, on our hearts, and on each person who will read this.

We have been blessed by the instrumental role that our families—Todd, Bennett, and Deanna—played by graciously supporting the early mornings of writing, jumping in with feedback and input, and constantly believing in the mission we are on to unhinder hearts and lives.

We are incredibly grateful to Dusty Rubeck and CDF Capital (cdf.capital/blessingranch) for financially partnering with us in this project. Their investment in helping churches and leaders thrive has allowed us to extend our reach with this transformational resource to so many. Their support has helped us accomplish so much more than we could have on our own.

Most of all, God deserves our recognition for being the "Senior Partner" in all our pursuits and endeavors. He leads us with wisdom, care, and strength. We are only capable of doing all we do because of the Holy Spirit within us, making us more than we are on our own.

—Charity Byers and John Walker

AUTHOR'S NOTE

I once had someone recount a dream he had in which he was speaking to a large crowd from a podium. When he looked down, he noticed a hole in the floor at his feet, revealing that he was standing on his father's shoulders as he spoke to the crowd.

That image has deeply stuck with me. I stand on my father's shoulders too. My father and co-author, John Walker, has spent forty years accumulating learnings from his work and personal walk with God that have influenced every word on the coming pages of this book.

Decades ago, the Holy Spirit began revealing to my father the concepts of the Unhindered model of transformation (found here and in the stand-alone *Unhindered: Aligning the Story of your Heart*). As he tuned in intently to what the Spirit was teaching him, he began to articulate the framework for emotional and spiritual growth and reengineering that you are about to learn.

When I share from my experience what I've learned about myself and what I've learned about what it looks like to join God on an incredible adventure of becoming, my father's fingerprints are all over each word, even when those words come from my perspective. I now have the privilege of furthering what he's begun.

I have been blessed by my father's steady obedience to stay willing to listen and learn from the Spirit. I hope you will be too.

Dr. Charity Byers

CONTENTS

YOUR INVITATION

You are invited to pursue an unhindered life, a life without the burdens, bad habits, and barriers that weigh you down, trip you up, or stand in the way of your next step. The unhindered life is the life you've always wishfully wanted but called impossible. Whether you didn't know how to get it or you didn't believe in it, there is a pathway for you to follow to find it—and that's what this book is all about.

Over the span of thirty days, you will be led through a defined process of opening up your inner world to heal and grow so that a better version of you can show up in your family, your community, and the world. This isn't about pipe dreams coming true. This is about stepping into greater emotional and spiritual health to allow you to make that impact you always wanted to make while being free of that weight that has always made life feel harder than it should.

The ultimate purpose of pursuing an unhindered life is to get yourself out of the way (all the things within you tripping you up and holding you back), so you can do two primary things: 1) follow God and not yourself and 2) be available to serve and love others well. A life with Jesus is not about self. It's about our surrender to Him and our service to others.

However, the oxymoron is that you have to be self-aware in order to get self out of the way. Some of you might come from a world that has taught you that it is selfish to pay attention to yourself. As a result, you have suppressed your own needs in order to serve others. There are some of you that might have come from a world that taught you that you must defend, rely on, and focus on yourself to be successful. The pathway to an unhindered life doesn't include either self-denial or self-focus. Rather, it's about entering into the tension between the two that truly allows you to get self out of the way and live and love as God intended.

The pathway toward an unhindered life first requires you to embrace self-understanding and shed self-denial. You have to pay attention to your heart! You have to give your heart the attention it requires to come to know what's inside of you that makes you do what you do, think what you think, and feel what you feel. Self-understanding then allows you to manage and take control of the internal, unwanted influences that keep misguiding and bringing out the worst in you instead of the best.

The pathway to an unhindered life also requires you to take self out of center view. Some put self in that position because of pride. Others do it more unintentionally as their own pain, insecurity, fears, or trauma keep their emotions overwhelmed to the point they can't think about anything but how things impact them and what they need to do to be okay. Submitting your heart to a healing and growth process with God is the answer in either case. Dealing with the root that has elevated self can put self back in its rightful place.

When we get self out of the way, we become unhindered.

Your unhindered self is your healthy self. Your healthy self is able to match your actions with your faith and follow God's lead and not your own. Your healthy self matches your love for others with the way you actually treat others. Your healthy self is available to make the difference you are meant to make and leave a positive mark on the people and places you touch.

Ultimately, your unhindered self is strong. This strength helps you stay secure, rooted in trust and hope through the challenges that come your way, and helps you have the faith to keep getting back up when life tries to knock you down. Strength allows you to say "no" to all the unwanted influences and allures within you and say "yes" to the life God imagined for you when He formed you.

Your unhindered self is a closer reflection of who God intended you to be. An unhindered life is the life God intended you to live— not easy or perfect, but full of perseverance and purpose.

This adventure you're invited on, to pursue an unhindered life, may push you. It may make you uncomfortable. It may make you feel like you don't have the answers you need. Step into discomfort and even confusion until you get to the other side. They may be necessary companions to bring you into the strength and freedom that wait for you. Always remember that you are not alone. God is always with you. And so is everyone else joining you on this adventure toward an unhindered life.

An unhindered life calls your name. Will you say "yes" to the adventure?

YOUR COMMITMENT

Unhindered: Thirty Days is meant to be read alone and then ideally shared in a group setting where there is ample time to process what you are reading. This process of finding your pathway to healing will take being vocal and vulnerable. As you read, if you feel you need to dig deeper into the material or want some further explanation of a concept you encounter, check out the book *Unhindered: Aligning the Story of Your Heart* for more. It is available at availleadership.org/unhindered or amazon.com.

Maybe you have never investigated the contents of your heart. Maybe you have been doing the hard, heart work for years now. Or maybe you are scared to death about what pain this might cause to resurface.

Let me encourage you to take one day at a time. Each day will lead you to the next step, so don't try to overthink what is coming around the next corner.

Let me also suggest that you commit time daily to accomplish all that this experience entails and asks of you. You will benefit from this the most by not packing in the information but by slowly absorbing it each day and then processing it alone and with others.

If you are processing this experience with a group, please use the "GROUP QUESTIONS" at the end of each week to guide your discussion. The questions are meant to pull together your learnings from all five days of your personal reading and reflection and help you begin to share the contents of your heart's story. Be sure to give space for each person in the group to be able to share, and encourage everyone to be as vulnerable as they can be.

I know that we are all busy, but remember this is our invitation to make time for ourselves, our hearts, and our healing. This is not just hard work—this is also holy work.

Before you begin, make a commitment to God, yourself, and each other (if doing this in a group setting) to do the work and show up for each other.

You can even sign your name below as a personal reminder that you are fully committed to this experience.

I commit to myself & this experience...

Signed

BEFORE YOU BEGIN

On the next few pages, you will notice some of the icons from the front and back covers that will hopefully become very important to you as you read this book.

These icons are from the model of heart transformation that will guide your journey. Each icon corresponds to a specific piece of the model and will remind you of the heart work that God can do at each phase to align you more with Him. Following the models are glossaries that define each piece of your heart's story.

You'll be learning more about each of these concepts over the span of the next thirty days. Refer back to the model and glossaries any time you need a quick reminder of a concept or to reflect on how each piece of your story fits together. As you read, the model and the icons will make more sense, and it is our sincere hope that they help bring healing, freedom, and power to your life and story.

THE HINDERED HEART

A story written by flawed authors, compromising our ability to live freely and lightly. Living in a hindered narrative stalls your heart's emotional and spiritual development, producing a misaligned heart that revolves around yourself and your own life experiences.

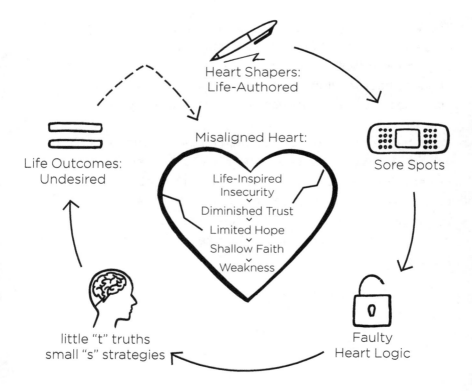

Heart Shapers: Life-Authored

The multidimensional influences that mold the shape of our hearts. Negative influences and impacts leave a mark on our hearts that don't align with God's design for us.

Sore Spots

The bruising or site of a wound in our hearts left by a negative Heart Shaper that becomes a filter within us, shaping (often unknowingly) our feelings, perceptions, and actions.

Faulty Heart Logic

Our heart answers "no" or makes exceptions about the goodness of God, ourselves, others, and/or life. Those answers set a faulty foundation for our more detailed thinking and doing in life.

little "t" truths

Our experiential truth that appears true because we've seen it, lived it, or felt it.

small "s" strategies

The things we do in order to try to be okay or feel protected, given the distorted reality that a little "t" truth has created.

Life Outcomes: Undesired

The undesired impacts on our lives (emotional, relational, spiritual, behavioral, physical, character) that result from the contents of our hearts being misaligned.

Misaligned Heart

A hindered heart that is insecure, unable to trust and hope, move forward in faith, and have strength to overcome, endure, and love.

THE UNHINDERED HEART

A story edited by God, giving us the ability to live freely and lightly. Becoming unhindered matures our hearts' emotional and spiritual development, producing aligned hearts that revolve around God's healing, freedom, and power in each piece of our stories.

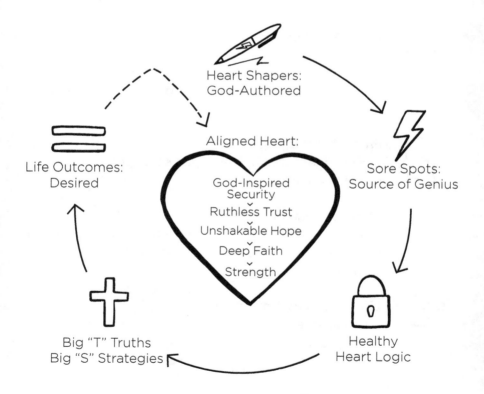

Heart Shapers:
God-Authored

Life Outcomes:
Desired

Aligned Heart:
God-Inspired
Security
⌄
Ruthless Trust
⌄
Unshakable Hope
⌄
Deep Faith
⌄
Strength

Sore Spots:
Source of Genius

Big "T" Truths
Big "S" Strategies

Healthy
Heart Logic

Heart Shapers: God-Authored

When the multidimensional influences that have molded the shape of our hearts, in the past, no longer have power because God's influence and authorship have taken their place.

Sore Spots: Source of Genius

The very best of us that shows up when a Sore Spot is healed by God and turned into purpose.

Healthy Heart Logic

Our heart answers "yes" about the goodness of God, ourselves, others, and life. Those answers set the healthy foundation for our more detailed thinking and doing in life.

Big "T" Truths

God's perspectives and realities (Truth) that lead us into health and abundance.

Big "S" Strategies

The postures and actions God intended for us that lead us into health and abundance.

Life Outcomes: Desired

The desired impacts on our lives (emotional, relational, spiritual, behavioral, physical, character) that result from the contents of our hearts being aligned with God.

Aligned Heart

An unhindered heart that is secure, able to trust and hope, move forward in faith, and has strength to overcome, endure, and love.

WEEK 1:

The Heart

DAY 1

Hindered

*Therefore, since we are surrounded by such a great
cloud of witnesses, let us throw off everything that
hinders and the sin that so easily entangles. And let us
run with perseverance the race marked out for us.*
—HEBREWS 12:1

"Open your mouth." This is a challenge that God gave me a few years ago, and it still defines my intention every day. It did not come easily, and it still does not some days. My historical "normal" was to listen and follow, be overly cautious with my promptings and opinions, and avoid saying too much so I would not say the wrong thing.

I was held back for so much of my life by an insecurity deep within me that kept me from seeing myself the way God sees me. That insecurity weighed me down and held me back. And with that insecurity guiding my heart, people-pleasing, following the leader, denying my own intuition, and staying in the shadows became my life.

I was existing.
But I was not fully alive.

I was content.
But I was compromised.

I was hindered.

That insecurity only led me to a life of hiding by convincing me that it was safest to hide. For much of my life, hiding seemed to work. Until it didn't.

There are chasms between who we are now and the best or optimized version of ourselves.

When I developed an alcohol problem in college, I obviously hid that too. It seemed convenient (for myself and for others), but hiding what hinders us is always dangerous. Because I hid, I chose to battle alcohol entirely alone and in my own strength. I compromised my character, trust with people I loved most, and my ability to face God without shame. My "safe" place of hiding had now fully exposed a gap between the life I pretended to live and the life I was actually living. A gap was also exposed between the life God desired for me and the life I had resigned myself to live.

If you have ever been on the London Underground in the United Kingdom, then you have probably been reminded to "mind the gap" by an automated recording or visual cue as you prepare to step from the station platform onto the train. It is a warning to pay attention to the gap between where you stand (on the platform) and where you want to go (the train).

We need to mind the gaps in our lives too. There are chasms between who we are now and the best or optimized version of ourselves. There is distance between our lives as they are and the beautiful, impactful, purposed lives God envisioned when He created us.

In *SoulTsunami*, Leonard Sweet said, "What is the difference between a living thing and a dead thing? In the medical world, a clinical definition of death is a body that does not change. Change is life. Stagnation is death. If you don't change, you die. It's that simple. It's that scary."[1]

Change. Is that an exciting or scary word to you? With God, change is an invitation to actually experience the abundant life— more peace, joy, passion, connection, fulfillment, contentment, and no hiding. It's an invitation to see the best of you, the unhindered you, show up each day, and make an actual difference in the world around you.

How do we change? How do we partner with God to bring out the *optimized* version of ourselves?

Hebrews 12:1 calls us to "throw off everything that hinders and the sin that so easily entangles and run with perseverance the race marked out for us."

This verse is clear that sin stands in our way. We must get the blatant things out of our life that bring darkness, secrets, and damage to our lives, but we also must "throw off everything that hinders." So what hinders us other than sin?

Other weighty interferences found in our hearts—many of which we pay little attention to—can also greatly hinder us. Some interferences could be insecurity, self-doubt, a need for control, fear of failure, being cynical of others, a mistrust in God's love, or expectation of life turning out a certain way. These hindrances in

---

1   Leonard Sweet, *SoulTsunami* (Grand Rapids: Zondervan, 2009).

our hearts do not separate us from God as sin does, but they also do not reflect the character of God.

I cannot imagine my life today had I resolved to live my life being "voiceless." As God took me down a path of finding my voice, He showed me what He truly wanted from me. God asked me to open my mouth so that He could use me to stand beside and breathe life back into those who are battle weary. He asked me to help Him realign hearts with truth that would set others free. For too long, I would have remained hidden and would have been too hindered to say "yes" to God.

There is distance between our lives as they really are and the beautiful, impactful, purposed lives God envisioned when He created us.

Do not settle for a hindrance within you. If you are living hindered, you are compromised and not fully alive. Maybe you are already very much aware of what your hindered life looks like. For others, maybe you are still questioning what hindrances could stand in your way of full living.

A hindered life might leave you vulnerable to the overwhelming voice of anxiety that will not shut up.

It might lead you to become a workaholic to impress others while your marriage and children suffer.

It might cause you to overextend yourself because you are too afraid of disappointing others, eventually burning out and quitting.

It might tell you to hold everyone at arms' length to protect yourself and feel safe, maybe even including those who genuinely love you.

It might make you a perfectionist, a rule-follower, and one who is resistant to living in the freedom of God's grace.

It might have you on your computer viewing sites you know you shouldn't because you are not willing to face abuse from your past.

If you don't relate to these situations, do not make the mistake of assuming you are not hindered. Stay curious about your heart, and let God show you what abundantly waits for you.

Too often, we are blinded by our normal and justify our hindrances by saying, "This is just who I am." But there is so much more that God wants us to experience in the abundant (dare I say, unhindered) life.

More ease. More impact. More emotional and spiritual health. More strength to rise beyond your circumstances. More alignment with God's desires for you. More of a difference to make.

I challenge you to throw off everything that hinders so you can run the race before you with perseverance.

Prayer:

(If you feel comfortable, open your palms to signify surrender and pray the following prayer).

God, show me how I'm hindered. Is there any sin that I am hiding from you? Reveal to me any interferences that I have been settling for in my life that hold me back from alignment with you. I desire to step out of just existing and being complacent. I want to stop being compromised and partner with you to experience the true freedom you promise. I open myself up to the work that you want to do in me to align my heart with yours. Amen.

Reflection Questions:

Is there any sin or hindrance that you are trying to hide (or manage on your own) from yourself, those closest to you, or from God?

Do you feel that there is a gap that needs closing in your life between where you are now and where you feel God wants you to be?

What is standing in the way of you closing this gap and fully living?

What stood out to you most in today's reading?

God is inviting you into a new normal to throw off the sin and hindrances that are keeping you from the abundant life that He desires for you.

Blinded by Normal

Choose your rut carefully. You'll be in it for the next 400 miles.
—FROM A SIGN IN THE AUSTRALIAN OUTBACK

We often live in a rut, blind, and usually blissfully unaware of it. We are blinded by our normal because when it is all we have known, it becomes all we can see and expect. Our life experiences and journey can become all that makes sense to us.

A client named Michelle shared this story with me:

I didn't know that people talked about feelings until I went to college. Until then, I thought the only appropriate conversations were the weather, what I'm learning in school, and what we have on the calendar this week. My family did not talk about anything that really mattered. We dealt with the blows of life by looking on the bright side. We ignored our irritations and grievances between us so we could keep the peace. I pretended so long that I ended up numb and oblivious to what was happening inside of me.

When I got to the dorms the first semester, and I heard people calling each other out for things they didn't think were right or heard them share their vulnerabilities, I was blown away. I literally did not know people did this! Up to that point, my normal was my normal. All I knew was pleasantries and peacekeeping. This new way of vulnerability and authentic connection scared me and excited me at the same time. I had no idea how to step into the vulnerability and emotion that was before me. And quite honestly, I didn't know if I wanted to. It was just easier to ignore my heart than to face my heart.

Too often we live helpless to the hindrances in our life because we have no idea that we are even hindered.

Michelle had been so blinded by her life experience, her normal, that she didn't even know there was something wrong, something hindered. She didn't know there was something more, something better.

Too often, we live helpless to the hindrance in our life because we have no idea that we are even hindered. We are just going about our normal life. It may seem good enough, but in reality, we have settled for less. We're blind to the gap between where we are and the life God intends for us to be living.

Some of us actively choose our normal because it has become comfortable. We stay fiercely faithful to the known, even when it is not worth our loyalty. While that insistence on comfort may minimize pain, challenge, or change in the moment, it compromises us in the long run.

Sometimes, we will recognize that we're discontent or we're hurting, but we don't know the way out, so we make the hindrance our friend. We turn a blind eye to the gap between what we desire and what we are actually living while doing our best to cope or numb our way through it. It never works as well as we think it does, and we end up compromised there too.

Michelle's emotional maturity was compromised. She didn't know how to unhinder her own heart, so the intimacy of her relationships was limited. She felt too awkward and unsafe to go deep with anyone, so she served them, not allowing herself to be fully vulnerable and loved. Her spiritual health was hindered too. Her relationship with God was reduced to obedience and keeping the peace, instead of opening herself up to fully experiencing His love and peace.

Will you keep living your normal? Or will you get curious about what more there could be?

Here's what you risk by denying the "curiosity of more" and simply living in your "normal."

- *You might risk inadvertently saying "no" to the Holy Spirit.*

  "There is much more we would like to say about this, but it is difficult to explain, especially since you are spiritually dull and don't seem to listen" (Hebrews 5:11).

- *You might risk living with this deadly phrase, "This is just who I am." It is a paralyzing declaration of resignation.*

  "Being confident of this, that he who began a good work in you will carry it on to completion until the day of Christ Jesus" (Philippians 1:6).

- *You might risk relationships as you expect everyone else to adjust to your unhealthiness and make it their problem.*

  "Why do you look at the speck of sawdust in your brother's eye and pay no attention to the plank in your own eye?" (Matthew 7:3).

- *You might risk living enslaved to a problem and spending your energy justifying it rather than fighting it.*

  "What shall we say, then? Shall we go on sinning so that grace may increase?" (Romans 6:1).

Our normal might feel comfortable, but it can be selfish. Our normal might feel safe, but it can be limiting. Our normal might feel easy, but it might be sinful. Our normal can feel painful, and it doesn't have to be! Blinders off; there is MORE!

My friend Lisa leads a wonderful organization called Amplify Peace. Part of what she does is take people on global immersion trips who may have been blinded by their normal. She intentionally tries to disrupt the unexamined narratives others hold about a people group, politics, history, faith, or life, by creating opportunities for them to sit face to face with people from all sides of a conflict or divide to hear their stories. She wants to help people stop their normal (blind) assumptions and bring awareness to the narratives of the misunderstood, forgotten, and overlooked. She believes it makes us more like Jesus.

As she shared with me what compels her work, she said, "You can't *unsee* what you've seen." There was no normal to go back to after her first trip to Israel and Palestine. She could never *unhear* their stories or *unsee* their faces. This has become *the more* that God had for her. She now invests her life into this mission to disrupt other people's normal, creating more room for compassion, peace, and grace in our world.

Along our way in life, God will present moments that can challenge our normal, like the story you just read. Or like Michelle's story, where she encountered something outside her box—openness, emotion, vulnerability. Both women didn't know whether they wanted to embrace what they had seen or run away from it. I'm grateful they both chose to embrace.

Will you keep living your normal? Or will you get curious about what more there could be?

Because it is so foreign, too often, we try to ignore what challenges our normal. We disregard the moment that God is using to desperately try to get our attention. Those moments are meant to snap us out of our resignation and self-justifications. They are meant to show us that another way is possible. They are supposed to lead us to self-evaluation and even repentance sometimes.

What will you do when something challenges your normal?

Maybe it will come from a friend who says, "Did you know that you can say "no"? Maybe it'll be the example of someone at work who does something you admire but seems so out of reach to you. Maybe it will be the stirring of the Holy Spirit that opens your blind eyes to something you can't *unsee* and keeps you awake at night.

When you see something or someone that exudes more freedom, peace, surrender, selflessness, or courage than you have, I hope you won't try to *unsee* it.

I hope you become curious in that moment and ask, "Is this really the way God intended for this to work?" "Is there more that I am not seeing?"

I hope you are willing to hold everything loosely, surrender what feels safe and protective, and say, "I am yours to mold, God. I trust you to show me there is another way."

This I know for us all: there is more beyond our normal.

This I know for us all: there is more beyond our normal. More courage. More intimacy. More obedience to God. More joy. More self-control. More well-being.

Take God's invitation to believe that He can bring you out of your normal, whether it's comfortable or painful. You can trust Him to make a way whether you can see a way out or not.

Prayer:

God, I surrender my normal to you. I lay all I have known at your feet. I surrender my comfort to you. At the cross, I leave all I have depended on for life to feel predictable, safe, and successful. I surrender my justifications to you. Into your hands, I offer my excuses and rationalizations. God, open my eyes. Give me the curiosity to see what more I can experience in you when I ruthlessly trust your heart for me.

Thank you for being a God who always has more for me. Amen.

Reflection Questions:

What normal do you feel God challenging you to see with fresh eyes?

What "more" do you feel that God is showing you?

Do you have the courage to pursue it with Him?

What stood out to you most in today's reading?

If we get curious about our hearts, we will realize that God is inviting us to step beyond our normal into more.

Why Should I Care?

The pursuit to unhinder our hearts already seems like a lot of work, doesn't it? Are you thinking about how much easier it would be to just live in the normal and stay hindered even if your normal is not good?

Are you thinking about all the other ways you could spend your time or all the other people you could help instead?

Are you thinking about how selfish it is to care so much about your own heart or your own impact?

We live with all kinds of myths that tell us that attending to our hearts is not worth it or it's not possible:

If I slow down and deal with myself, I will get overwhelmed by it and won't be able to get going again.

What is the point if I don't know the way out?

It is too selfish of me to pay attention to my soul. Others need something more from me right now.

I'm supposed to have it together as a grown-up! I can't believe I'm still dealing with this issue after all these years of walking with Jesus.

If I admit this hindrance, it makes it too real. I can't face that right now.

I can't afford attention to this right now. I can't get distracted from all that God has called me to do.

Unhinder your heart to unhinder your life.

Even though I know this isn't the healthiest way of doing it, I'm coping with it, so I must be fine.

You *must* get these myths out of your way so that you can pay attention to your heart. Everything depends on it! That might sound dramatic, but it is very true.

Proverbs 27:19 affirms, "As water reflects the face, so one's life reflects the heart."

You must unhinder your heart to unhinder your life.

The freed heart that God imagined for you is unlocked from the oppressive fear, anger, discontentment, or unsettledness to lead you into the freedom, joy, and impact waiting for you. But your hindrance is making you stop one step short of it.

God does not stop one step short of *anything*.

- *He didn't stop creating until He could declare it all as good.*

  "God saw all that he had made, and it was very good" (Genesis 1:31).

- *He didn't stop one step short of our redemption by saving Jesus from the cross.*

  "For God so loved the world that he gave his one and only Son, that whoever believes in him shall not perish but have eternal life" (John 3:16).

- *He didn't stop one step short in creating you.*

  "I praise you because I am fearfully and wonderfully made; your works are wonderful, I know that full well" (Psalm 139:14).

God doesn't want you to stop one step short either.

Here are a few things He wants for you:

1) Optimized Joy and Peace:

Jesus meant it when He said, "I have come that they may have life, and have it to the full" (John 10:10).

If you feel enslaved to pain, heartache, conflict, angst, or anxiety, God lovingly wants to release your heart from these burdens. You may not be able to change your circumstances. It may be that God wants to help you live by the unseen, not the seen. He invites you to fix your eyes on Him and the hope, love, security, and belonging He can give you that this world cannot. Do you believe that God wants a full life for you?

2) Optimized Impact:

You are the light of the world—like a city on a hilltop that cannot be hidden. No one lights a lamp and then puts it under a basket. Instead, a lamp is placed on a stand, where it gives light to everyone in the house. In the same way, let your good deeds shine out for all to see, so that everyone will praise your heavenly Father. —Matthew 5:14-15 (NLT)

We cannot stop one step short of letting our light shine into the darkness. There is something that only *you* can do in this world. There is someone who needs to hear *your* voice. There is a mission that needs *your* gift. Have you held yourself back in places where God has called you to bring light?

3) Optimized Character:

The fruit of the spirit (Galatians 5:22-23) gives us a glimpse into the heart God desires us to live from when we are emotionally and spiritually well. Love, joy, peace, patience, kindness, goodness, faithfulness, gentleness, and self-control are not meant to be separated from one another.

If we have given ourselves a pass on one or more of the fruit of the spirit by saying something like, "I'm doing pretty well by being kind and gentle, so my lack of self-control isn't such a big deal," then we're stopping one step short. We must live with the fullness of the fruit of the spirit to be a true ambassador for Christ in our families, communities, and churches. Have you made excuses for your character?

4) Optimized Strength:

Hebrews 11 is a chapter of strength. It tells the stories of faithful followers who had two kinds of strength:

Some had strength to overcome challenges and adversity.

> *By faith these people overthrew kingdoms, ruled with justice, and received what God had promised them. They shut*

the mouths of lions, quenched the flames of fire, and escaped death by the edge of the sword. Their weakness was turned to strength. They became strong in battle and put whole armies to flight. —Hebrews 11:33-34

God does not stop one step short of anything.

Others had strength to endure suffering and persevere even when they had no victory.

There were others who were tortured, refusing to be released so that they might gain an even better resurrection. Some faced jeers and flogging, and even chains and imprisonment. They were put to death by stoning; they were sawed in two; they were killed by the sword. They went about in sheepskins and goatskins, destitute, persecuted and mistreated. —Hebrews 11:35-37

If our faith is not making us emotionally and spiritually strong, something in our faith is wrong.

We need the kind of strength that comes from unshakable faith to overcome or endure a challenge that doesn't seem to end. We need the kind of strength that does not let circumstances like success, victory, and desired outcomes either prove or disprove the reality of faith, just as these heroes of the faith had in Hebrews 11.

Have you stopped one step short of the strength that will allow you to have hope, trust, and resilience even when your circumstances don't show you a good reason to have them?

5) Optimized Alignment with God:

"My old self has been crucified with Christ. It is no longer I who live, but Christ lives in me. So I live in this earthly body by trusting in the Son of God, who loved me and gave himself for me" (Galatians 2:20).

Living a life with Christ is all about living surrendered. Surrendered to His will. Surrendered to His commands. Surrendered to His chosen outcomes.

When we are hindered, instead of surrendered, we can become too self-involved. And even without meaning to, we end up obstinate, saying "no" to God more than we realize. We get overtaken by our own logic and compulsions that our heart justifies to stay safe. We can't hear the whisper of the Spirit telling us to take the risk because our fear is too loud. We can't fathom forgiving that person because our anger will burn anything it touches. We can't trust someone that God has put in our path because we're too "gun shy" from our repeated disappointments.

God doesn't want you to stop one step short either.

There's grace for our hindered hearts. They are just so limited by what they have seen and lived that they can't even entertain what God is offering them. God is not shaking His head in disappointment at us for being hindered. He is inviting us to throw off what hinders us and to align ourselves with all that He has for us. Do you believe that with God is where it's truly safe?

This is God's invitation:

Unhinder your heart to unhinder your life. God does not stop one step short. He doesn't want us to stop either.

Prayer:

God, show me what myths have stopped me from examining my heart and bringing it before you. Holy Spirit, show me where I could be stopping one step short from the optimal life you have created for me. Rid me of myself, and help me surrender all that I've known. Thank you for your grace. Thank you for this invitation. Amen.

Reflection Questions:

Go back and answer the questions at the end of each Optimization section:

1) *Optimized Joy and Peace*: Do you believe that God wants a full life for you?

2) *Optimized Impact*: Have you held yourself back in places where God has called you to bring light?

3) *Optimized Character:* Have you made excuses for your character?

4) *Optimized Strength*: Have you stopped one step short of the strength that will allow you to have hope, trust, and resilience even when your circumstances don't show you a good reason to have them?

5) *Optimized Alignment* with God: Do you believe that with God is where it's truly safe?

What stood out to you most in today's reading?

Don't stop one step short of unhindering your heart so that you can experience the freedom and fullness of life that God longs to bring.

It Begins in the Heart

You cannot save a dead bush by trimming its branches. You must dig out the rotted roots and allow God to replant new life in place of the old.

Have you spent too much energy dealing with the dead branches instead of the roots? Have you spent too much time waiting for your circumstances or for other people to change when it is you that needs to change?

So many people come into a marriage counseling session armed with all the things they need their spouse to do for their marriage to be better. "If she would stop being so critical, I'd be nicer." "If he would pay more attention to me, I'd have sex with him more." While they often have some legitimate complaints about each other, it never goes anywhere until they are willing to disarm and take a deeper look at themselves.

We all tend to think that the solution to our problem is to change our circumstances. Change our spouse. Change our schedule. Change the amount in our bank account. Change the amount of time in a day.

Changing these external things may help for a moment. It might create some short-term relief. But that discontentment, distrust, dissatisfaction, or dread will likely follow you wherever you go.

Let's be clear—it's not all your fault! Other people do need to change sometimes! I'm just saying that the most lasting way to be well is to change your own heart toward the circumstance.

We all tend to think that the solution to our problem is to change our circumstances.

Even when we're in unrelenting circumstances or when someone around us is doing a lot of damage, our hearts can still experience freedom from the fear, shame, resentment, and anger if we make the choice to surrender our hearts to God instead of our circumstance.

Your heart is your ticket to freedom.

We can learn a lot from Scripture about the heart. The word *heart* is used 570 times in the NIV Bible, and it is most often used metaphorically to describe the inner self, just as we're defining it, the place where feelings, thinking, longings, and willpower meet. The biblical writers often refer to the heart as the place of our personhood, our true selves.

Proverbs 4:23 says, "Above all else, guard your heart, for everything you do flows from it."

The heart is the source of life. It is the reason you do what you do, say what you say, and think what you think.

Did you know that your heart is that critical? Not only is it capable of giving life by pumping blood through your body, but it is also capable of giving life through holding an identity rooted in Christ. This produces thoughts that align with God's thoughts and desires that match God's desires.

It is also capable of stealing life from you when it is burdened by pain, fear, shame, pride, and self-indulgence.

Our hearts get misaligned with God by all the things we experience in this life that don't reflect God. These are the rotted roots that God longs for us to dig up: the abandonment we felt as a child or as an adult, the constant judgment we cast on ourselves, the mistakes and sin we hold over our heads, or the trauma that robbed our sense of safety.

When we invite God into our circumstances, pain, moments of disappointment, relationships that have left us wounded, and confusion we feel in times of uncertainty, He can bring our hearts back into alignment with His. He can fill us with His presence, perspective, kindness, and love that breathe new life to the dying parts of our souls.

It all begins in the heart. Let's not wait for change. Let's invite change. Give credence to the heart as the source of life to find true freedom and allow God to work.

Your heart is your ticket to freedom.

"The Spirit of the Lord God is upon me, because the Lord has anointed me to bring good news to the afflicted; He has sent me to bind up the brokenhearted, to proclaim liberty to captives and freedom to prisoners" (Isaiah 61:1, NASB).

Prayer:

God, help me pay attention to what matters most—my heart. I invite you to expose the rotted roots within my heart and bring new life. I believe that you are the healer that can breathe life into my weary heart and soul. You are the binder of my broken heart. You are the freer of the places, spaces, circumstances, and people that I have held captive. I give you access to my heart, God. Amen.

Reflection Questions:

Do you find yourself waiting for something around you to change, and it never does? Is your heart burdened and stealing life from you while you wait?

How might you experience that ongoing challenge differently if you adjust a perspective or posture in your heart?

Are you willing to invite God into these places?

What stood out to you most in today's reading?

Lasting change comes from acknowledging that we cannot always change our circumstance, but we can surrender our hearts to God and be changed in the middle of that circumstance.

Partnership with God

No discipline seems pleasant at the time, but painful.
Later, however, it produces a harvest of righteousness
and peace for those who have been trained by it.
—HEBREWS 12:11

G *od, just get me out of this!*

God, fix this! I can't do this anymore!

God, help me wake up tomorrow and not face this ever again!

How many times have you prayed these kinds of prayers out of desperation? Or maybe out of demand?

I know that I prayed many prayers like that going through my battle with alcohol. I wanted to be rescued, and I also wanted God to erase my memory so that I would never be plagued by the shame of remembering what I am capable of.

We long for ease. We long for a quick fix. We long for God to do what we know He can do—a miracle!

Whether we are trying to get out of a sinful pattern we are stuck in, maybe urgently waiting for the rescue of someone we love, or desperate for the strife of a situation to end, we so often want-pray-beg for instantaneous relief from God.

God most definitely deserves our praise for the miracles He has done and is still doing. We know that He can do the unthinkable in an instant because we have read that Jesus raised Lazarus from the dead

Any good partnership helps us accomplish things we can't do on our own.

(John 11:38-44) and turned water into wine (John 2:1-11)! Miracles are still happening! People have told me incredible stories, such as getting a check from a random stranger for exactly the amount they owed for an unpaid bill or cancer vanishing inexplicably from someone's body.

While He's truly the God of miracles, He's also the God of training.

Training is a process, not a moment.

These stories of training are all over the Bible. Here are two examples:

- Luke tells us about ten lepers who asked Jesus to heal them in Luke 17:11-19. "He told them, 'Go show yourselves to the priests.' On their journey, they were cleansed" (v. 14). Only one returned to thank Jesus, but all ten were healed when they took steps of obedience.

- John describes a scene when Jesus and the disciples passed by a man who had been blind since birth in John 9:1-6. The disciples (like most of us) immediately wanted to find the cause and pin the blame. They asked, "Rabbi, who sinned, this man or his parents, that he was born blind?" (v. 1). Jesus explained that God had bigger plans than they knew. He made some mud from dirt and spit and told the man to wash in the Pool of Siloam. He did, and he received his sight. The man had to take action for the miracle to happen.

The lepers were commanded to do something in the process of healing: *"Go show yourselves to the priests"* (Luke 17:14). As they partnered with Jesus in the process, they were healed. The blind man had to wash in the Pool of Siloam. When he took part in the process, he was healed. What did they gain through having a part to play? Perhaps more faith? Perhaps more trust in Jesus? Perhaps more gratitude for the gift?

God needed to train me *through* my battle with alcohol. I'm certainly not suggesting that He incited the problem to teach me a lesson, nor that He prolonged it to make a point. I hold responsibility for the darkness I let into my life, and all God ever wanted to do was to have me back as His. In His infinite wisdom, He knew that the best thing for me during that process of returning to full relationship with Him, was to have to wrestle with some things. Without that wrestling, I'd be left too vulnerable in the future. Not just to alcohol, but to a life with things in the shadows, possibly even pitch-black darkness.

God needed me to join Him in creating the miracle. You guessed it. He needed me to stop the life-long pattern of hiding I'd developed out of my insecurity. He needed me to break the secret and expose myself. He needed me to face my shame with the gift of witnessing first-hand the power of grace in action—the kind of illogical grace that can only exist because someone's heart is so sold out to Jesus. He needed me to get over my self-reliance and let Him and others help.

What a kind God! A God who loves us so much and longs to take away our pain and struggle, but also a God who knows that the best thing He can do is seize the moment that offers the training we need to look more like Him when it's through.

There are some universal things that God trains us in as we endure. He wants us to learn to have a deeper trust and dependence on Him. We only do those things to the degree life really requires of us. When God allows us to stay the course in something hard, we must stay desperate for Him every day. We must learn that we cannot control it or fix it, so we must learn to trust God too. Sometimes God has personal training for us. Sometimes He breaks us of a lifelong pattern or addresses a very personal faith struggle in our story.

God wants to partner with you in the deep transformation of your heart.

It does not always feel good during the training process. Hebrews 12:11 says, "No discipline seems pleasant at the time, but painful. Later, however, it produces a harvest of righteousness and peace for those who have been trained by it."

Training can be painful. But it is always purposeful.

Think about those Navy Seals who bear freezing water and physical torture to prepare for their missions. They endure such physical pain and emotional agony to be ready to deny their needs, fear, or dangerous instincts when mission time comes. It's so painful, but it's purposeful.

Training wasn't pleasant for me either. I was incredibly uncomfortable, squirming in my seat in fact, as I had to admit things out loud that I didn't even want to admit to myself. But all of this led to stepping into the unknown waters of vulnerability, letting others in more deeply, learning to turn the volume down on the voice of shame, and clearing my heart out so that I could let God restore and have more.

Do you want to know the best part about this training process? We get to do this *with* God. When we are being trained, we certainly have a part to play, but God isn't throwing all the work off on us either and saying, "Good luck with that." Not at all. God invites us into partnership. We do not have to do this on our own. Nor do we need to demand that God do it without us. We get to work together. Another beautiful outcome of training is the union we can feel with God when we've gotten through it together.

The other good news? Any good partnership helps us accomplish things we can't do on our own.

In my story, I could not have beaten alcohol without God. He gave me supernatural courage to break the secret. He sent people around me to show me grace that helped quiet my shame. I even believe He tempered future temptations that I would have expected to be so much worse. With His help, I could heal. With His help, I could become a closer version of the woman I think He intended me to be.

In Matthew 11:28 (*MSG*), God lovingly says, "Walk with me. Work with me. Watch how I do it. I won't lay anything heavy or ill-fitting upon you." Let those words wash over you and remind you that you can trust His training process. No matter how painful, I challenge you to believe this training is purposeful.

If God wanted to immediately free you or heal you, He would have already answered your prayer. Instead, He might want to walk *with* you and show you things that you would not learn from complete and instantaneous relief.

God wants to partner with you in the deep transformation of your heart. It will not be quick, but it will be better than you've ever imagined.

Prayer:

God, I want to partner with you to unhinder my life. I surrender my desire for a quick fix and instant change. I commit to walk through the process of healing and growing with you so that I may be strengthened by it.

Use these training grounds to make me more like you. Teach me to depend on you more. Teach me to trust you more. Free me from the hindrances of my past.

Show me the part I must play. Help me to trust you to do your part. Together, may we accomplish what I cannot do on my own. Amen.

Reflection Questions:

What circumstance (shame, sin, addiction, or hurt) are you currently asking God to take away from you? Will you step into the pain it brings, believe that a process of growth and healing is purposeful, and allow for God to partner with you in the midst of it?

What reactions do you typically have when things aren't resolved immediately? Are you annoyed and impatient or trusting and surrendered?

Are you dependent on God in the midst of your circumstance or are you dependent on your circumstance to determine how you will trust and depend on God?

What stood out to you most in today's reading?

Our training is purposeful. It is how we learn even greater trust in and deeper dependence on a good God.

WEEK 1: GROUP QUESTIONS

1) Where is there a gap that needs closing in your life between where you are now and where you feel God wants you to be?

2) What "normal" do you feel God is challenging you to see with fresh eyes? What "more" do you feel God is showing you?

3) Select and share the questions that spoke the most to you in the "Optimized" section of Day 3:

Joy and Peace: Do you believe that God wants a full life for you?

Impact: Have you held yourself back in places where God has called you to bring light?

Character: Are you conscious of striving to have the fruit of the spirit in your life, or have you made excuses for your character?

Strength: Have you stopped one step short of the strength that will allow you to have hope, trust, and resilience even when your circumstances don't show you a good reason to have them?

4) Is there something in you or around you that you have desperately wanted to change, that might require you to adjust a perspective or posture in your heart?

5) Are you dependent on God during your circumstance or does your circumstance determine how you will trust and depend on God?

WEEK 2:

Heart Shapers & Sore Spots

The Shape of Your Heart

"**S**ecretariat is widening now! He is moving like a tremendous machine!" The announcer's incredulity transcended through time as he bellowed, "Secretariat by 12, Secretariat by 14 lengths . . . an unbelievable, an amazing performance!"[2]

The racehorse, Secretariat, won the Belmont Stakes by thirty-one lengths in 1973 to secure the Triple Crown. This record-smashing performance, among other record-setting performances that still stand today, were largely made possible by the incredible shape of his heart.

Secretariat's heart was estimated to be 21 to 22 pounds, which is 2.5 times larger than the average horse. "Secretariat's unusually large heart enabled him to receive more oxygen, allowing his muscles to receive optimum oxygen replacement for faster recovery, therefore increasing his stamina. He continued to run faster with each stride he took due to this phenomenon." His heart "acted

---

2   Chic Anderson, CBS commentator, June 9, 1973.

like a V8 engine in a sports car" and paired so perfectly with his broad girth and perfected muscles.[3]

Secretariat's heart was in great shape, and optimum performance was made possible by an optimum heart. You certainly need your physical heart to be in good shape because it will have an immense impact on the quality of your life. Will you be able to spend quality time with your grandchildren one day? Will you be okay to take that trip you have always wanted to go on with your spouse? Will you be able to fulfill the dreams that God has given you? There is no doubt that we know that the heart is important.

Remember, Proverbs 4:23 tells us, "Guard your heart for every-thing you do flows from it."

Do you give enough credit to how imperative it is to have your heart in good shape!

We are charged by Solomon to pay close attention, maintain, care, and offer support to our hearts. The heart that he is talking about is more than just the organ that pumps and circulates blood in order to keep us alive; it is the very soul and personhood of our spiritual being. Thinking through this lens about your heart, do you give enough credit to how imperative it is to have your heart in good shape?

Scripture tells us that paying attention to the shape of your heart determines the shape of your life. So how do you determine the shape of your heart?

3 M. Boggs, "Secretariat: TWICE the Heart: Veterinarian Swerczck Shares the Untold Story," Kentucky Equestrian Journal, (January 2020), issuu.com/equestriandirectory. ensoimedia/docs/ked-2020/s/10168613.

Just as chest tightness and shortness of breath might signal us to check on the shape of our physical hearts, our souls offer us warnings when they are in trouble. Maybe you have experienced or are experiencing withdrawal, unwanted anger, uncharacteristic moods, intrusive thoughts, hypervigilance, constantly second-guessing yourself, or many more signs that alert you that your heart needs attention.

The shape of your physical heart has been influenced by things such as how much heart-healthy food you eat, the quality of your exercise, and also by your genes (if only we could control that!).

The shape of your soul and personhood has been influenced by two things: your DNA and your life experiences.

Your DNA has primed you with personality and inclinations. Your heart has also been powerfully shaped by what you have encountered and experienced in your life. Author Reggie McNeal said, "While God is in the heart shaping business, so much more than God has shaped your heart."[4]

Some of us may be born with a personality or inclination that gets amplified by life experiences. A person wired with drive may turn into a workaholic when praise only comes for good performance. The person wired for peace and harmony may become more afraid of conflict when anger invades their home. The person wired for creativity may become adamant about having freedom to pave their own way after their family tried to box them into their own expectations.

While there are definitely some valuable new healing opportunities in the process of encountering God, we know that choosing faith does not mean the complete and instantaneous abandonment

---

4 Reggie McNeal, *A Work of Heart: An Expository Study of 1 Corinthians* (Hoboken: Jossey-Bass, 2000).

of every unhealthy, impure, and painful influence and experience outside of God. We still carry with us the impacts of our life story that have shaped our hearts.

This is where the journey begins. We get to join God as we are, trust Him with all of our story, and let Him become the only one who shapes our heart. This takes time! It takes intention! It takes the power of the Holy Spirit! If you have been living a life of faith but your past has been hidden for fear of what this means for you as a believer, you are being invited right now to unhinder your heart.

This is a loving invitation from God to lay out all the pieces of your soul and allow Him into each and every part. Jeremiah 18:6b says, "As the clay is in the potter's hand, so are you in my hand." Even though our imperfect lives and experiences have hindered our hearts and put things in them that don't belong (selfishness, bitterness, judgment, self-indulgence, fear, and mistrust), God is still the potter who longs to return your heart to the optimum shape He intended (joy, peace, hope, confidence, security, and patience).

Just as chest tightness and shortness of breath might signal us to check on the shape of our physical hearts, our souls offer us warnings when they are in trouble.

You are not a stagnant being—only capable of who and what you are right now. You are not limited by what your personality type on the latest self-assessment tool says you are inclined to be. You are not reduced to a product of where you come from, what you have been taught, and what has been modeled for you.

Let God reshape your heart. Allow Him, and Him alone, to determine the shape of your life.

We still carry with us the impacts of our life story that have shaped our hearts.

Prayer:

God, show me the shape of my heart. Reveal to me where my soul is hungry and thirsty for more of you. Show me where I have settled for mediocrity and where I have not been diligent to care for the shape of my heart. God, please help me on this journey of understanding what has shaped my heart. Amen.

Reflection Questions:

What kind of shape is your heart in? Are you experiencing withdrawal, anger, uncharacteristic moods, intrusive thoughts, hypervigilance, constantly second-guessing yourself, or any other warning signs that your heart needs attention?

What is it like to hear that so much more than God has shaped your heart (i.e. DNA and life experience)?

What thoughts come to mind about people or events that have shaped your heart?

What stood out to you most in today's reading?

The shape of my heart
is not just determined by
its physical shape —
but so much more by
the health of my soul.

Heart Shapers — Looking Back

Dear children, keep away from anything that
might take God's place in your heart.
—1 JOHN 5:21 (NLT)

Experience can be a great teacher when it comes to matters of skill. If you are trying to learn how to hit a baseball, there is no substitute for stepping up to the plate and feeling the way the bat connects with the ball. But experience is so often an unreliable teacher in matters of the heart.

My friend has spent the last few years trying to unhinder her heart after being shaped by sexual abuse from a teacher. As she stepped through the door of her school every day, it was not a safe place. She felt alone, unprotected, and one moment away from seeing the sickening view of his face around the corner. The familiar fear crept in: *Where is he? Has he seen me yet? How will he try to corner me today? What if someone finds out what I've done?* She learned something through those years of fear. *You are the only one here to look out for you, so don't trust anyone and stay in control.* Long after the days of abuse were over, she could not shake what she had learned. The

Experience is so often an unreliable teacher in the matters of the heart.

abuse had shaped her heart and taught her heart to fear. Her heart did not know how to let go of being in control of everything, everyone, and every outcome. She was living hindered.

My heart rips in two as I imagine how living with fear became her normal. Trapped by her secret, with only herself to guard against him, hypervigilance became her weapon. Being on guard, being in control, holding tight to trust, and finding ways to numb her anxious heart became her insulation from the fear. Fear, control, and mistrust are not things God would have wanted in her heart.

God had an intention for what your heart should look like, but lovingly, God turned your heart over to be a part of this world. He honored the choice that Adam and Eve made for all mankind—to depart from a life protected from sin and evil (Genesis 3). This is the gift of free will that He has given us. Even though it does not seem to make much sense for God to turn us over to brokenness and sin and willingly let anything other than Him shape our hearts, it makes perfect sense when you think about the end goal. When God gives us full and utter freedom to choose to follow Him, true relationship with Him is made possible.

God allows our hearts to experience things in this world that don't look, sound, or feel like Him. Experiences can bring us rejection, while God is always full of pursuit. Experiences can bring judgment against us, while God is always full of grace. Experiences can bring abuse, while God is full of tenderness. Experiences can bring unmet expectations, while God is full of security. Our hearts have learned by experience. And while experience can feel true and even more real than God, experience can be such a bad teacher!

All of the multidimensional influences that mold the shape of our hearts are called *Heart Shapers*. All of us have a blend of Heart Shapers that include drama, tragedy, love, and even some comedy, but for many, the stories have far too much drama and tragedy. Remember how Reggie McNeal put it, "While God is in the heart shaping business, so much more than God has shaped your heart." Some Heart Shapers are experiences that have happened to you. Other Heart Shapers are things that are within you.

Primary Heart Shapers are things that we can see and grasp, like experiences and moments. Secondary Heart Shapers are more subtle influences that modify Primary Heart Shapers, like beliefs and emotions. (You can see more examples of Secondary Heart Shapers in Appendix A). In this book, we'll pay most attention to our Primary Heart Shapers.

Here are some of the primary things that shape our hearts:

1) *Biology.* Defined by your nature, personality, physical characteristics, and DNA.

    Negative examples: a disability that impacts your experience and identity, a predisposition to depression or anxiety, a driven nature

2) *Family.* The lessons, patterns, and impacts derived from a family of origin that have long-term effects.

Negative examples: sibling rivalry, absent parent, explosive anger in the home, harsh or inconsistent family rules, abuse, abandonment, critical environment

3) *Everyday life experiences.* Moments that may not stand out individually but accumulate into messages that matter and shape our hearts.

Negative examples: a relationship ending, losing a job, disengaged spouse, repeated criticism, unattainable expectations, enduring a narcissist

4) *Defining Moments.* Individual events that have an extremely strong impact for good or for bad. These can include "God moments" and mountaintop experiences as well as traumatic events.

Negative examples: abuse, divorce, infidelity, death, major illness, significant loss

5) *Sin/Evil.* Your sin, others' sin, and spiritual warfare that continue to shape your heart as you face circumstances, make decisions, and experience daily life.

Negative examples: giving in to temptations, moral failures, sinful thoughts, impact from the sins of others

The heart takes in all of the information from these influences and stores it, synthesizes it, and ultimately makes meaning from it. When something has enough force behind it, it shapes your heart. It can be an instant that changes your trajectory for a lifetime, or sometimes it is repeated, dull pain that happens over and over, making it hard to ignore the message. No matter how you get there, Heart Shapers either shape God's intentions for your heart, or they distort the truth of God's love, forgiveness, power, and joy, leaving you insecure, frantic, and defensive.

The shape of your heart begins to form early in your life. In fact, many experts say that the trajectory of our emotional life is shaped in the first three years of life.

As I stated earlier, I was a shy kid. Shyness did not just happen to me—it was a part of me. It wasn't just a decision—I was created to be that way. It came naturally, but I also locked myself in that box with the dangerous self-judgments I made.

The perceived perfection in my parents shaped me also. It seemed to me that they never had a bad day. They didn't seem to ever make mistakes, so I decided I wasn't supposed to either. I feared vulnerability, especially with them. I learned to hide and "fake it," and as you now know, that proved to be a dangerous plan when it came to struggling with alcohol.

Maybe in your story, you have had someone's critical voice eat away at your confidence.

All of us have a blend of Heart Shapers that include drama, tragedy, love, and even some comedy, but for many, the stories have far too much drama and tragedy.

Maybe for you, it has been the constant disappointment of people who say they love you, but their betrayal has stolen your trust.

Maybe for you, it was the continually changing expectations someone had that robbed you of security outside of your performance.

Maybe for you, like my friend, it was an experience that shaped the way you see all people and life.

Here's the invitation for you! Begin to connect the dots in your story. You will have to look backward before you can look forward. Many of us avoid naming the reality of our past out of fear of slandering or judging others. Remember that this process of naming your Heart Shapers is about understanding, not judging. Your insight into your early life will be the crucial beginning of your awakening.

> Heart Shapers either shape God's intentions for your heart, or they distort the truth of God's love, forgiveness, power, and joy, leaving you insecure, frantic, and defensive.

What has shaped your heart other than God? What influences and experiences have been in your life that have taught you something that competes with God's Word? Where did you learn to reject others before they can reject you? Where did you learn to be so critical of yourself? Where did you learn to expect the worst-case scenario to come true?

Don't miss the chance to tell the story of what has shaped your heart by being too quick to dismiss the shaping power of your life. Many of us like to think we have moved on from things that happened decades ago. But our hearts remember. Many of us like to think we're strong enough to not let it get to us. But our hearts' instincts will still betray us. Many of us like to think that if we really trust God, there's no need to examine our pasts. But true trust means trusting God with all of it.

You will have to look backward before you can look forward.

When you get curious about what has shaped your heart, you can begin to tell the story of what life has put in you that God did not. It is the beginning of disrupting your normal and choosing to partner with God to unhinder you from all that has held you back.

The true beauty of God's design in sending us into a broken world is that He is right there to put our hearts back in the shape He intended when we choose to partner with Him. God is right by our sides to give us an alternative to what life has taught us. He is there to remind us of how He delights in us, how much we can trust His unfailing character, and how to see hope beyond our dreary circumstances again. Most of us are just too blind or too busy to give God that opportunity.

It's hard to reshape what life has shaped, but it is NOT impossible with God. Be ready for a fight. The old does not give up easily.

Prayer:

God, I give you all of my past and present. Bring to mind the Heart Shapers that you want to redeem in my life. Help me get curious and bring these to you for healing. I believe that you care about me and are in full pursuit of my heart. Amen.

Reflection Questions:

Have I lived with the belief that nothing from my past impacts my life now?

Take time to journal your Heart Shapers. (There is a timeline provided for you in Appendix A, with examples.) Ask God to bring to mind events, pleasant and painful, that have shaped your life. Feel free to look back at the list of primary things that have shaped our hearts (Family, Everyday Living, Defining Moments, Biology, Sin).

What stood out to you most in today's reading?

I have to look backward before I can move forward. So much more than God has shaped my heart.

DAY 3:

Sore Spots — Shaped by Pain

"That's going to leave a mark." I have said that plenty of times after running into the corner of the desk while trying to read a quick email as I walk into the next appointment. (You've been warned. It's dangerous to walk and read at the same time!)

Most painful things leave a mark, and I've had plenty of bruises to show for my blind encounters with those sharp desk corners.

Your hearts have marks on them too, showing the times they've been hurt, disappointed, left unprotected, unfairly judged, and run over in your life.

When you experience Heart Shapers that do not reflect God's love, wisdom, and strength, and they leave painful bruises on your heart, we call them *Sore Spots*. It's the site of your wound—the place where pain has made a home. Sore Spots are the bruises our hearts carry as evidence of living in this imperfect world, where things other than God shape our hearts.

A Sore Spot might feel painful and tender, but it might not feel very sore at all, perhaps numbed by the passing of time or being distracted, so you don't have to pay attention.

Even if your memory has faded and your pain has numbed, your heart remembers.

In my conversations with people over many years, I have seen the same Sore Spots over and over again. They surface in six primary ways:

- *Shame:* Feelings of overwhelming guilt, embarrassment, or believing you deserve blame. Shame causes you to see things that go wrong as your fault and incites self-condemnation.

- *Fear:* Feeling out of control or unprotected; experiencing undue worry and pervasive anxiety. Fear leads you to consistently expect the worst and want to protect yourself.

- *Inadequacy/Insecurity:* Feeling like you're not enough or that you don't measure up. Feelings of inadequacy and insecurity cause you to doubt your abilities. They make you believe others are condemning you or are disappointed in you.

- *A sense of rejection:* Feeling like you don't belong and aren't wanted. You see yourself as expendable, cast aside, or dismissed.

- *Feeling unvalued:* Feeling unimportant, forgotten, unworthy, or overlooked. This perception causes you to feel minimized, overlooked, and despised. It creates self-perceptions of inferiority and insignificance.

- *Pride:* Feeling superior to others or being overly self-focused. Pride makes you see only success in yourself and failure in others. It inflates your importance and exaggerates your perception of others' admiration for you.

These may or may not be words you typically use to describe yourself. For many, these Sore Spots remain unnamed and covered up by secondary or surface-level emotions like frustration, anger, or disappointment. You have to strip away your defenses and dig down to the roots of your heart to actually see a Sore Spot.

Even if your memory has faded and your pain has numbed, your heart remembers the impact as if it were yesterday. That means that Sore Spots can hinder you long after the relationship ends, the abuse stops, you finish school, leave the church, or you grow up and get out of your parents' house.

Just as Heart Shapers introduced this pain to your heart, Sore Spots then introduce the pain into your life.

Just as Heart Shapers introduced this pain to your heart, Sore Spots then introduce the pain into your life. Hearts with unmanaged Sore Spots lead us to feel, think, and act in ways that do not reflect God. Our hearts don't mean to be disobedient (most of the time!). They have just one goal: don't feel any more pain. The heart full of fear wants to feel safe at all costs. The heart wounded by rejection wants to justify its loneliness. The heart bruised with shame wants to minimize and compartmentalize the pain.

You know you have a Sore Spot when you start feeling like the apostle Paul who said, "I don't really understand myself, for I want to do what is right, but I

We all have triggers.

don't do it. Instead, I do what I hate" (Romans 7:15, NLT). When something happens that hits our Sore Spot, we react—often in ways we don't like. We react out of self-protection. Our instincts kick in, raise their voice, and insist: *Don't let anything make you feel what that Sore Spot feels ever again!*

A good indication of an unrecognized Sore Spot is a disproportionate emotional response to a person or situation—either overreacting or underreacting. Overreacting is when someone blows up in anger or bursts in tears at a relatively minor event. Underreacting is the lack of normal, healthy emotions. In these cases, someone has numbed out to avoid the discomfort of the Sore Spot.

We all have triggers. They are the things that turn us into someone we don't recognize. They are the things that leave us scratching our heads asking, "Where did that come from?"

We get triggered when our Sore Spots get hit by something that happens in our lives today that threatens the pain of the past.

Here's the perfect example that happens in marriages all the time. Kim shares something she'd like Tom to improve on. She tries to do it nicely and calmly. (She despises conflict by the way.) But regardless of her approach, what she gets back from Tom is defensiveness. Without even realizing what's happening inside of him, Tom is automatically defending himself against his insecurity being proven true. He responds to Kim by immediately deflecting blame and responsibility. He turns the tables to point out all the things she does that compare to or beat her complaint.

The seemingly easiest way for Tom to not feel insecure is to level the playing field by bringing Kim's character on par to his (or lower than his).

It didn't even matter that Kim was trying to be helpful. Tom could not handle ownership in the moment because it was too threatening to his Sore Spot of insecurity. He couldn't act maturely or respectfully. He couldn't make it safe for Kim to share things with him; instead, he shut her down. His Sore Spot hindered him and intimacy in his marriage.

"Why do I keep doing this?" "Why do I keep holding back when I really want to be more deeply connected to people?" "Why do I avoid applying for a new job when I can't stand what I'm doing?" "Why do I keep working too much even though I'm so tired all the time?" "Why do I feel like I have to control everything all the time?" "Why do I get so angry about something so small?"

Are we all just crazy?

Are we all just crazy? No, we have Sore Spots in our hearts which have significantly shaped our life's storyline. Every moment of every day, our Sore Spots hinder us, almost certainly more than we realize.

Prayer:

God, you have seen every day and every piece of my story. You know the events and experiences that have shaped something in me that isn't from you. I believe that as I open my heart up to painful places I might usually avoid, you will meet me and redeem each and every part. Thank you for holding every piece of me in your hands. Amen.

Reflection Questions:

Where do I find myself underreacting or overreacting? What is the Sore Spot attached to this emotional response?

What feeling have I numbed or avoided in an effort to keep pain away?

Allow the Holy Spirit to be your guide as you look back at your list of Heart Shapers from yesterday. See if you can match a Sore Spot to your five Primary Heart Shapers. (They are listed for your convenience in Appendix B.)

What stood out to you most in today's reading?

My heart has sore spots left by the pain and imperfection I've encountered, and those sore spots hinder my life.

DAY 4:

The Filter

O ur Sore Spots are like an unseen, unwanted force inside that is silently manipulating us.

It is like the parent who has you as the puppet on their string, even when you don't know it! They masterfully convince you that you don't want to play football because you're more of a soccer guy (even though mom and dad are just afraid of you getting hurt). They tell you how wonderful it will be to live at home during college, so you don't have to do your own laundry (just because they are not ready to let you go). They are so good at making you think it was your desire and instinct the whole time that you do not even stop to question it. That's exactly what your Sore Spot is out to do.

When there's an unhealed Sore Spot reigning in your heart, it will be your interpretive guide. It will tell you how to see things, what to believe, and even what to do. But instead of unleashing you, it will hinder you.

Your Sore Spot creates a confirmation bias, so you see only what you're looking for—not what's really there. Your filter has a seemingly magnetic energy that attracts what fits the Sore Spot and rejects what doesn't!

If your Sore Spot is rejection, it seems that rejection is waiting around every corner. If your Sore Spot is insecurity, it seems that everyone is judging you and accusing you of doing a terrible job. If your Sore Spot is fear, you will see threats everywhere. When your heart filters life through the Sore Spot, you don't (and can't) see things as they really are.

Our Sore Spots are like an unseen, unwanted force inside that is silently manipulating us.

When you can't see clearly, you don't feel accurately either. Sore Spots can be full of emotion, and the intensity of emotion can lock you into biased narratives, lead you to misinterpret others' hearts, and cause you to receive the wrong feedback from others. Because the Sore Spot is so convincing, feelings are accepted without evaluation as the beacon of truth. Too often, we end up hiding behind this imperfect logic, *If I feel it, it's true.*

You experience a cascade from the way you think and feel to the way you act. The cloudy perspective that your Sore Spot gives you, coupled with the physiological activation and subjective experience of emotion, takes you off course, and you make unwise decisions. You skip the critical step of evaluation: "Should I listen to myself?" Without considering that your heart has misguided you, you let the dominant message from your Sore Spot propel you into action.

When Sore Spots take over part of God's intended story, God's truth is stuck in your head as knowledge. It can't live in your heart where it shapes good and godly actions. Almost certainly, your Sore Spot compels you to make choices that you don't want to make. It creates a glass ceiling that limits your ability to take the next step. Your Sore Spot keeps you from fully living out the purposes of God.

Ten men who traveled to the land of Canaan over three thousand years ago may have had the unwanted influence of a Sore Spot shaping their encounter. In Numbers 13 and 14, we read the story of twelve scouts who were sent by Moses to explore Canaan, the land promised to the Israelites, and bring back their observations. Moses wanted to know what they were up against as they prepared to take the land. He wanted to know whether the people there were strong or weak, whether the land was fertile or poor, and if the land was protected or unprotected (Numbers 13:17-20).

The twelve scouts reported back to Moses after forty days. Based on the conflicting stories, you would think he had split the scouts, sending them in two different directions. Two of the scouts, Joshua and Caleb, reported that Canaan was a "rich land flowing with milk and honey" (v. 8b). They said of the people of Canaan, "They are only helpless prey to us! They have no protection, but the Lord is with us! Don't be afraid of them" (v. 9b)! Joshua and Caleb saw promise, hope, and victory.

The other ten scouts saw doom and defeat. Their picture wasn't just one shade off; it was completely contrary to what Joshua and Caleb had seen! The ten reported, "The land we traveled through and explored will devour anyone who goes to live

When you can't see clearly, you don't feel accurately either.

there. All the people we saw were huge. We even saw giants there, the descendants of Anak. Next to them we felt like grasshoppers, and that's what they thought, too" (v. 32b-33).

All twelve had seen the same things. How could some see an easy victory while others saw giants? How could some see milk and honey while others saw a land that promised to devour them?

This wasn't just a case of optimism versus pessimism. This wasn't just Caleb and Joshua looking on the bright side while the others were pessimistic. Something was empowering the lens of the ten scouts: the unseen impact of a Sore Spot.

The ten scouts who saw doom may have had a Sore Spot filtering their perspective. Do you remember what they'd been through? They had been slaves their whole lives! Maybe their enslavement (a Heart Shaper) had created a Sore Spot of helplessness. Imagine the impact of having no control, being overpowered, and constantly being a victim. Perhaps slavery had left them with defeat and "we can't" written on their hearts. As they looked out on the land of Canaan, helplessness may have been their filter. That is why they saw normal people as giants, and their misperception made them feel small and vulnerable like grasshoppers.

Your Sore Spots keep you from fully living out the purposes of God.

What about Joshua and Caleb? Surely slavery took its toll on their hearts, too. Either they made it through slavery without a Sore Spot purely by the grace of God, or they had already redeemed their Sore Spot with God's help. As they looked out over the land of Canaan, their hearts were running on trust and hope in God rather than hopelessness and defeat of their lives as slaves. As they saw Canaan through God's perspective, they were able to see the potential, the possibility, and the promise of the land God was giving them. To Joshua and Caleb, it looked like the land of milk and honey because it was.

They compel us to do things we wish we didn't do or paralyze us from action when God says "go."

When we look closely at the ten spies in Numbers 13 and 14, we also see how their Sore Spots may have filtered their emotions as they viewed the land of Canaan. If it's true that the slave life they had experienced left them with fear and defeat as Sore Spots, they would have been overwhelmed with more fear and defeat as they looked at the land and the people. A sense of helplessness could have caused them to feel incapable, perhaps convincing them the land would "devour" them (v. 32b).

But Joshua and Caleb were filled with excitement and possibility. Their confidence and hope gave them eyes to see "a rich land flowing with milk and honey" (v. 8b).

It's a safe bet that the ten scouts' Sore Spots told them to go home. That was not God's plan and Caleb didn't listen to them. He was a man of action. He insisted, "Let's go at once to take the land. We can certainly conquer it!" (Numbers 13:30b). Caleb and Joshua were ready to charge ahead with God's plan for action because they didn't have hopelessness and defeat written on their hearts. Even if they had moments of doubt, hope and victory were able to dominate.

Sore Spots get in our way. They take away our ability to see what God sees. They lock us into feelings that seem right but are only a reflection of the old pain that's getting triggered in the moment again. They compel us to do things we wish we didn't do or paralyze us from action when God says go.

Their influence is in our way of the health, strength, and love we so desperately want.

Sore Spots have to go. Their influence is in our way of the health, strength, and love we so desperately want.

This is your promise: "He heals the brokenhearted and binds up their wounds" (Psalm 147:3).

Let God heal your Sore Spots.

Prayer:

God, help take the blinders off as I continue to dive into the Sore Spots that have hindered my life. Show me the ways in which you wish to restore the feelings and emotions that did not come from you. I trust you with my heart and I believe that hope and victory are on the way for me. Amen.

Reflection Questions:

Look back over your Heart Shapers and Sore Spots you have written down and identified. What is God pressing you to notice about them right now?

How have your Sore Spots affected the way you think, feel, or act? What have they kept you from?

What difference do you think it will make if you trust God to heal your Sore Spots?

What stood out to you most in today's reading?

Your Sore Spots can take away your ability to see what God sees and do what God wants.

Your Source of Genius

P astor and author Tim Keller observes,

Christianity offers not merely a consolation but a restoration—not just of the life we had but of the life we always wanted but never achieved. And because the joy will be even greater for all that evil, this means the final defeat of all those forces that would have destroyed the purpose of God in creation, namely, to live with his people in glory and delight forever.[5]

God wants—no, He longs—to heal the Sore Spots in your heart, fresh or dulled, big or small.

Stop pretending the pain isn't there so you can let God show your heart what life couldn't—His grace, love, and truth. As God touches your pain, your Sore Spot begins to lose its influence.

---

5   Tim Keller, *Walking with God through Pain and Suffering* (New York: Riverhead Books, 2013), 159.

God wants you to trade:

Shame for righteousness (Romans 5:1)

Fear for safety (Psalm 16:8, Joshua 1:9)

Insecurity and inadequacy for God-given esteem (2 Corinthians 3:5, 1 Peter 2:9)

Rejection for significance (Matthew 18:12)

Unvalued for cherished (1 John 4:19, John 1:12)

Pride for humility (Ephesians 4:2, James 4:6, James 4:10)

Will you trust God with your Sore Spot? When you consider this question something inside you may be yelling, *Are you crazy? Why would I dredge all that pain up again?* Almost certainly, you'll have to manage an internal civil war between fear and faith.

Will you trust God with your Sore Spot?

Listen to God call you into the safety of His presence. Listen to Him offering to wrap His loving arms around your heart and place His love where pain once reigned. Your reaction may be more along the lines of, *Why would I spend any energy searching for Sore Spots to heal when I'm fine?*

You need to remember that sometimes Sore Spots can be a silent, unseen manipulator. Don't get out-maneuvered by your own heart! You'll risk missing the discovery of what comes alive in you or gets unlocked when you trust God with your Sore Spot.

A wise seminary professor commented to his students: "The problems you suffer during the first half of your life become the source of your impact for the rest of your life." We agree, and we say it this way: "Your Sore Spots can become the source of your genius."

The disciple Peter had a Sore Spot. He was the first called to become a disciple of Christ. He dropped everything, including his career as a fisherman, to follow Jesus. He was part of Jesus' inner circle and showed how sold-out he was through these words, "Even if I have to die with you, I will never disown you" (Matthew 26:35).

But when pressure came, Peter caved. He denied knowing Jesus—his leader, his teacher, his Savior, his friend. When Jesus was arrested, we can only imagine the fear that rose up in Peter. The Gospels tell us that Peter reacted by grabbing a sword and taking a swipe at one of the men who had come to arrest Jesus. Thankfully, the fisherman wasn't too skilled with a sword. He cut off the man's ear. Jesus reminded Peter why He had come, and He reattached the man's ear.

God not only uses the site of your wound to bring out greatness in you but also through you.

When Jesus was taken for a trial before the Jewish council, Peter went along and waited outside. Several people asked him if he was one of Jesus' followers, but Peter realized that if they were going to kill Jesus, they were going to kill His followers, too! His instinct was to protect himself by lying. As Peter was questioned about his relationship with Jesus, he denied knowing him, not once but three times—all before the rooster crowed, just as Jesus had predicted (John 18:15-27).

When Peter realized what he'd done, his heart sank. A sold-out, committed disciple of Jesus had rejected him out of raw fear. Peter undoubtedly meant it when he told Jesus earlier, "I will never disown you."

What happened to Peter as a result of that denial? Imagine what could have been. You don't escape moments like that without your heart being terribly bruised. Scripture says that he broke down and wept (Matthew 26:75). Waves of shame washed over him. He may have felt that he'd lost the right to call himself a follower of Jesus. He had such grand plans to reign with Jesus in the new kingdom, but those dreams were shattered. Peter's denial bruised his heart, leaving a Sore Spot of shame.

When God meets us in our darkest places to comfort and strengthen us, He prepares us to touch other broken people with His love.

As we watch Peter's behavior after the denial, it's easy to imagine shame driving his actions. It filtered his self-perception, and it may have led him to give up on himself. In John 21:3, Peter says, "I'm going out to fish." Do you think that Peter's shame caused him to conclude that he was no longer part of Jesus' plans? Perhaps he saw himself as a failure and he resigned himself to the fact that his time of influence was over. Maybe he was thinking, *All I can be is a fisher of fish, not a fisher of men anymore.* Fortunately, that's not the end of the story for Peter. His genius, the best of him, was only waiting to emerge.

Jesus transformed Peter's Sore Spot. After Peter's denial and the crucifixion, Jesus appeared to the disciples several times.

One of these was when a group of them had gone fishing. After a miracle breakfast, Jesus took Peter aside. John's Gospel takes us to the scene:

> *When they had finished eating, Jesus asked Simon Peter, "Simon son of John, do you love Me more than these?" "Yes, Lord," he answered, "You know I love You." Jesus replied, "Feed My lambs." Jesus asked a second time, "Simon son of John, do you love Me?" "Yes, Lord," he answered, "You know I love You." Jesus told him, "Shepherd My sheep." Jesus asked a third time, "Simon son of John, do you love Me?" Peter was deeply hurt that Jesus had asked him a third time, "Do you love Me?" "Lord, You know all things," he replied. "You know I love You." Jesus said to him, "Feed My sheep." —John 21:15-17*

Jesus didn't confront Peter with fierce condemnation and words like, "You blew it!" Instead He asked, "Do you love me?" During those three strategic exchanges, Jesus wasn't actually trying to find out whether Peter loved Him. He already knew that. He needed to heal Peter's shame by helping him see that his love for Jesus was still real. When Jesus told Peter, "Feed my sheep," He was trying to get Peter to see that He loved him and still called him worthy. The conversation was about the redemption of shame. Jesus showed Peter that it is not about performance; it is about love. Jesus reminded Peter that he was still His disciple and a fisher of men.

Without this conversation between Jesus and Peter, we'd have to rewrite the book of Acts. After his Sore Spot was redeemed, we see a very different Peter—humble, yet bold. He preached the message on the Day of Pentecost and three thousand believed. In Acts 4, Peter and John were confronted by the Sanhedrin and questioned for healing a crippled man.

*Peter answered, "If we are being called to account today
for an act of kindness shown to a man who was lame and
are being asked how he was healed, then know this, you
and all the people of Israel: It is by the name of Jesus Christ
of Nazareth, whom you crucified but whom God raised
from the dead, that this man stands before you healed."*
—Acts 4:9-10

Peter had changed. He was
again defined by his God-
given identity instead of by his
mistakes. He was no longer a

*Surrender your
heart to God.*

shame-filled, discouraged man. He was confident and bold, with
security and redemption guiding his heart—he was unhindered.

Peter's shame could have been a threat to the future of the church.
What if he had given up on his apostolic calling? Jesus dissolved
his shame in the experience of love and security. That's how Peter
could be a major force in establishing the church! Ironically, Peter's
wound became the source of his usefulness, his impact, his genius.

Like Peter, the site of your wound can become the source of your
genius—the very best of you.

If we let God heal us and restore us, our Sore Spot will become
our strongest point. We'll have more wisdom because we've seen
God work when we were hopeless, we'll have more compassion
because we've experienced the depths of His grace, and we'll have
more strength because the Spirit's power has replaced our weakness. When God has worked, we can look back at the hardest times
in our lives with gratitude. Paul wrote, "We also glory in our suf-
ferings, because we know that suffering produces perseverance;
perseverance, character; and character, hope" (Romans 5:3b-4).

When your Sore Spot is faced and healed, you're released from the bondage of mediocrity, the paralysis of pain, and artificial limitations. You find yourself with a newfound depth to your spiritual and emotional maturity, filled with greater compassion, humility, love, and faith in God's power that couldn't have been produced any other way.

God not only uses the site of your wound to bring out greatness in you but also through you.

In a remarkable admission, the apostle Paul wrote that, at one point, he "despaired even of life." But God met him there, and he responded, "Praise be to the God and Father of our Lord Jesus Christ, the Father of compassion and the God of all comfort, who comforts us in all our troubles, so that we can comfort those in any trouble with the comfort we ourselves receive from God" (2 Corinthians 1:3-4).

When God meets us in our darkest places to comfort and strengthen us, He prepares us to touch other broken people with His love. If someone knows what it's like to be abandoned and alone, God's healing touch will make that person very sensitive to others' need for belonging. The healed person might be the only one to notice someone feeling uncomfortable and out of place at church and say, "Hi, I'm glad you're here." Those few and simple words have incredible healing power. The compassion we've gained from the redemption of our Sore Spots gives us the capacity to breathe life into the hearts of others. It helps us notice what others may miss. It gives us the conviction to act when others ignore a need or don't even notice it. And it gives us the ability to know just what to say to comfort the person's particular pain.

Your genius is waiting to emerge.

Our Sore Spots may not completely go away in some cases, but in all cases, they can be tamed and put in their place. Their power and influence can be taken back. With God, we can learn to take control of our hearts in the moment our Sore Spot is triggered and tries to take over. We can intently remind our hearts that God's truth is more real and true than the untrustworthy messages of life. We can turn up the volume on God's voice and let His affirmation, desire, comfort, promises, and love drown out the competition.

Surrender your heart to God.

Your genius is waiting to emerge.

Prayer:

God, thank you for your redeeming power. Thank you for the example of love and grace you showed to Peter. I know you offer that to me too. I offer my heart to you to be reshaped and remade so purpose can be made out of my pain. Thank you for promising to use everything for your glory and for good. Amen.

Reflection Questions:

How does Peter's story change how you see Sore Spots?

What part of your story are you willing to redeem?

How might a difficult part of your story become your source of genius?

What stood out to you most in today's reading?

When you let God heal your Sore Spot, your site of wounding can become your source of genius.

WEEK 2: GROUP QUESTIONS

1) What is it like to hear that so much more than God has shaped your heart (i.e., DNA, family, and life experience)?

2) Have you lived with the belief that nothing from your past is impacting your life now? Share some of your Primary Heart Shapers. (See Appendix A)

3) Share how you matched a Sore Spot to your five Primary Heart Shapers. (See Appendix B)

4) Reflecting back on your work, what has your Sore Spot kept you from?

5) How does Peter's story (from Day 5's reading) change how you see Sore Spots? How might a difficult part of your story become your source of genius?

WEEK 3:

Heart Logic

DAY 1:

Heart Logic — The Four Questions

Earlier, you were challenged to examine your Sore Spots and open your eyes to the influence they have on the ways you think, feel, and act.

This week, you are being invited on a journey to go much deeper into the impacts of the Sore Spots on your life. Over the coming weeks, you'll have the opportunity to unpack several distinct impacts on your thinking, feelings, and actions that flow out of the Sore Spots in your heart. This week, the unpacking begins with a laser-focused view on the most fundamental meaning you carry in your heart that can be influenced by your Sore Spot. It's called *Heart Logic*.

Small, seemingly innocuous things can pack a big punch. A dung beetle is not a glamorous insect and it's only a few centimeters long. It is, however, the strongest animal on the planet compared to body weight, with males being able to pull 1,141 times their own weight. That's comparable to a human pulling six double-decker

119

buses full of people. That's quite an impact coming from such a small thing![6]

Why are these questions so important?

Heart Logic is something within us that may seem small and innocuous too, but it actually packs a big punch. Our Heart Logic is the way our hearts answer four simple yet game-changing questions:

1) *Is God good? Is He really good all the time?*

2) *Am I good even though I'm flawed? Am I really valued and worthy of love?*

3) *Are other people good even though they are broken? Is there really goodness in humanity?*

4) *Is life good? Is life good even though it's so difficult?*

Why are these questions so important? How can such a big punch come from such basic questions? The answers we give either cement the foundation of our faith or they compete with our faith. As we answer the Heart Logic questions, we have three options:

1) *We say "yes." We see goodness the way God does, and our heart is aligned with Him.*

2) *We say "no." We see goodness the way our pain does, and our heart is misaligned with God.*

---

6 "Dung Beetle," *Wikipedia*, en.wikipedia.org/wiki/Dung_beetle.

3) *We say "yes, but..." That's really a "no!" We've made an exception or put a caveat on God's truth, and we're still misaligned with God to some degree.*

Healthy Heart Logic says "yes" to all four questions. Can you?

If you cannot confidently and unequivocally say "yes" to one or more of the questions, your faith gets compromised. You doubt when you really want to trust. You hold tight to control when you're being asked to surrender. You will shut out your godly community when you feel you cannot trust again after getting burned. You'll fall into depression when your hope is based on how well your life circumstances are going. Even if you have told others countless times how good God is and how much He loves you, are you aware of the struggle in your own heart?

It is also possible that these questions sound so simple that you're quick to say, *"Of course I believe that! Everyone knows that!"* But hold on! Don't be so sure you know how your heart has answered these four questions. Your heart's answers can be so different from your head's answers. Your head may know the "right answers," especially if you've been in church for a while or if you had healthy mentors or parents who reinforced these messages.

Healthy heart logic says "yes" to all four questions. Can you?

Nevertheless, if you give your heart a chance to speak, it might raise an objection or two. It might say, "I *want* God to be good, but what about . . . when my parent died suddenly, or my kid's tragic accident, or losing my job unfairly, or my illness that hasn't been healed." Sometimes, we just have too much competition from the Sore Spots in our hearts for what we know to be true to become what we experience as true. *Knowledge* and *experience* are two very different things.

We make sense of these questions with the logic our hearts provide—which is not really logic at all. Our heart's "logic" is really intuition and perception. The heart understands through experience and not reason—through perception and not rationale. That means that our heart's understanding doesn't always match our head's understanding. Jeremiah 17:9 affirms, "The heart is most devious and incurably sick. Who can understand it?"

> We don't bother to understand our answers, and that leaves us vulnerable to a lingering doubt that's never been challenged.

Our answers to the Heart Logic questions often stay unexamined and unexplored. We often don't even know that our hearts have answered the questions, but yet they have. We don't bother to understand our answers, and that leaves us vulnerable to a lingering doubt that's never been challenged.

Beginning quite early in life, our hearts take in information through all of our Heart Shapers and experiences, and they are assessing and creating meaning about what they encounter. During that process, if there's a Sore Spot filtering things that come in and out of your heart, then your perception might be compromised. You might not be able to see clearly, just like the ten spies from Numbers 13 and 14 that you read about earlier. They saw the land of Canaan as one that would "devour" them (v. 32b), while Joshua and Caleb (who it appears could see clearly without the influence of a Sore Spot) saw "a rich land flowing with milk and honey" (v. 8b).

So here's the reality. There are so many factors that influence our answers to these questions beyond our own reasoning. Pain, disappointment, trauma, and disillusionment found in our lived experiences influence our answers more than we would wish and more than we often realize.

I didn't stand a chance of answering the question, "Are you good even though you're flawed?" with any measure of conviction. I looked around the kindergarten classroom and decided the other kids had the right personalities—outgoing, friendly, and confident. I believed I had the deficient personality—the reticent, quiet, observer. With the influence of that insecurity (my Sore Spot) leading the way for my heart, there's no chance it was going to say, "Yes! I'm good even though I'm flawed by my shyness." The first mistake I would have made is calling shyness a flaw.

Years later, I found myself laced with shame and self-disgust because of the ways alcohol turned me into someone I didn't like at all. That Heart Logic question *really* didn't stand a chance of being answered "yes." My heart was misaligned with God because that "no" stole my ability to believe some portion of His truth.

When our Hearts have a Sore Spot in them, the answers to one or more of the four Heart Logic questions will likely be "no." With any "no," we lose capacity to experience and see things the way God intends, and that com-

Our faith is hindered by our Heart Logic.

promises a deep piece of security God intended us to have. Our faith is hindered by our Heart Logic.

But when we say "yes" to all four of the Heart Logic questions with conviction in our hearts and confidence in our voices, we get the chance to become spiritually and emotionally well. Four life-giving answers of "yes" align our hearts with God in a powerful way. We've said "no" to the experience-altering influence of a Sore Spot! Now we can see more like God sees! We are set up with a powerful foundation of truth that shapes and sculpts everything else within us—our daily thoughts, our choices, our go-to strategies, and even our Life Outcomes—to be a product of our faith.

There's so much power in four little questions. Begin to imagine the added richness that answering "yes" could bring into your life.

Prayer:

God, I want to unhinder my faith! Help me dive beneath the surface and look deeply into my heart for the answers to these questions. Help me be more honest with myself than I've ever been. Reveal to me the doubts and exceptions I've held that get in the way of believing in your promises. Thank you for patiently leading me. Amen.

Reflection Questions:

Be brutally honest and take some time to reflect on how your heart answers the four Heart Logic questions when you initially read them. Do you put any caveats on your answers?

How are your answers to the Heart Logic questions competing with your faith?

What stood out to you most in today's reading?

Your answers to the four Heart Logic questions either form the foundation of your faith or compete with your faith.

Dealing with the Exceptions

T hings in this life always seem to come with exceptions.

Learning grammar as a kid means having to carefully navigate the 10 percent of exceptions that seem to exist for every rule. It's confusing! When should we listen to the rule, and when should we disregard it? If you don't navigate the exceptions to a grammar rule correctly, it might hurt your English grade. But it most likely won't have major consequences for your life.

It's a different story when we're talking about navigating the exceptions to saying "yes" to the Heart Logic questions. In these matters, if we don't navigate the exceptions correctly, our faith and well-being are put at risk.

Remember the Heart Logic questions:

1) *Is God good? Is He really good all the time?*

2) *Am I good even though I'm flawed? Am I really valued and worthy of love?*

3) *Are other people good even though they are broken? Is there really goodness in humanity?*

4) *Is life good? Is life good even though it's so difficult?*

You know what's on the line. Answering "no" to any of the Heart Logic questions misaligns your heart with God and compromises your faith. Answering "yes" to the Heart Logic questions aligns your heart with God and catalyzes faith.

But it's just not that simple to say "yes" to the Heart Logic questions when some glaring exception of goodness you've encountered is all you can think about! And you're absolutely right that there are exceptions.

Not everyone is good. Sometimes you might encounter a truly evil person (even though it's important to be selective with that label).

> The exception does not change the rule.

Not everything about you is good. You do regretful things sometimes that do not look like faithfulness, gentleness, or self-control.

Not everything about life is good. You have to deal with injustice and heartaches that grieve and frustrate you.

It's not the expectation that you will have to adopt some ridiculous form of blind faith or naiveté in order to have healthy Heart Logic that's aligned with God. There are exceptions, and they must be dealt with. You must make room for them, but *do not* let them change your heart's starting place.

To be healthy and primed for faith, your heart's starting place needs to be, "Yes, God is good all the time, and I'm good even though I'm flawed. There is goodness in humanity, and life is good even though it's difficult."

With that affirmative starting place, we can embrace the exceptions as exceptions. That means the exception does not change the rule. The one evil person does not get the right to change our definition of humanity to untrust-worthy. The repeated sin in your life does not get to change your self-image to "only as good as my behavior." The fact is that too many of us start with "no" because of the exceptions.

Too often our instincts remember pain and disappointment far more than they expect good.

What happens when we start with "no"? Your heart is inadvertently fighting against your faith. Your heart will try to convince you to protect yourself by not getting too hopeful, being overly selective with your trust, and expecting nothing so you won't be disappointed again. Your heart is cut off from seeing and experiencing so much of the good that exists outside the exceptions.

The problem is that we just trust our normal too much. We rely on our first thought to be right. Too often, our instincts remember pain and disappointment far more than they expect good.

Even when it feels like pain and disappointment have been relentless and feel more like the rule than the exception, be careful to remember that there is always something more true than your experience—God's promises. God's promises of goodness are always the rule, even when it's hard to see that in your own life.

Faith won't ever require you to put on blinders and pretend the exceptions don't exist. Integrate the exceptions into your understanding, but don't let anything redefine God's truth. Be slow to trust your first thought and quick to trust your second thought. It's much more likely that your second thought will be driven by your faith and not your misaligned heart.

> *God's promises of goodness are always the rule even when it's hard to see that in your own life.*

When you start with "yes" and then leave room for the exceptions, you can find the hope and trust that will breathe life into your faith and help it become as natural to you as your own heartbeat.

Prayer:

God, you are so good. What you say is true. Despite what I might have experienced, help me put my doubts and exceptions in their place and stop letting them redefine you. Thank you for loving me and leading me into more hope. Amen.

Reflection Questions:

Have I allowed exceptions to speak louder than the truth?

Am I living with the truth as my first thought or my second?

What stood out to you most in today's reading?

The exceptions do not get to speak louder than the truth.

Rewriting Heart Logic

Second Kings 6:4-7 tells a story about a group of prophets who were building a new meeting place:

They went to the Jordan and began to cut down trees. As one of them was cutting down a tree, the iron ax head fell into the water. "Oh no, my lord!" he cried out. "It was borrowed!" The man of God asked, "Where did it fall?" When he showed him the place, Elisha cut a stick and threw it there, and made the iron float. "Lift it out," he said. Then the man reached out his hand and took it."

God made a heavy, iron ax head float to the surface. That's not supposed to happen! Heavy things do not float, especially a heavy iron ax head!

We serve a counterintuitive God, don't we? He doesn't play by our rules. He doesn't get constrained by the boundaries of logic. He doesn't feel limited by our capacity to know what to pray for. He does what we least expect, and He surprises us with unanticipated blessings. He makes the impossible possible and finds a way to bring goodness from tragedy.

It's not intuitive to expect an ax head to float. It's not intuitive to expect God to give up His only son to die an agonizing death on a cross. It's also not intuitive to say "yes" to the Heart Logic questions sometimes.

Our hearts have seen, lived, and felt things that do not align with trusting the goodness of God, ourselves, humanity, or life. We have tasted the bitterness of others' betrayal. We have ago-nized in our waiting as a prayer has gone too long unanswered. We have seen the stark look of disapproval on someone else's face. We have rehearsed the inner critic's degrading monologues countless times.

Experience is seen. Truth sometimes is unseen.

When we rely on the intuitive and the lived experience to define our reality, life is only as good as it is easy. People are only as good as they behave. You can only be as good as the good you do. God can only be as good as His outward blessings. Your well-being is tethered to the ebbs and flows of life, and you've given away your power to control your own joy.

But if we serve a counterintuitive God, and we are called to become like Him, then we're signed up to do the counterintuitive too!

God longs for your heart to unequivocally say "yes" to all four Heart Logic questions. Through that "yes," He wants to cement your heart in His truth, so it can become an even more reliable source of strength, wisdom, and wellness in your life. We're going to have to help our hearts along in the places they're opposed or just hesitant and unsure.

To do this, we're going to have to submit our intuition and sight to faith and truth.

Second Corinthians 4:18 (NLT) says, "So we don't look at the troubles we can see now; rather, we fix our gaze on things that cannot be seen. For the things we see now will soon be gone, but the things we cannot see will last forever." We are called to live by the unseen—the truth that stands as true, real, and trustworthy even when our experience doesn't match it.

Experience is seen. That means that what it teaches us feels intuitive to our hearts, and our hearts naturally lean into what experience wants them to believe is truth. One might have had a parent so inept in emotional maturity that they couldn't ever say, "I love you" out loud. Even with an unspoken message of love in the home, there's something missing in their experience that often casts a little doubt on how lovable they are. So what becomes intuitive? This message: *I'm not sure I'm enough to fully be loved.*

Truth sometimes is unseen. That means that its realities can feel incredibly counterintuitive to our hearts. They feel like competition to our experience, and the tangible experience often feels more real and true because it's seen. Unfortunately, that's the wrong conclusion. Nothing is more reliable, everlasting, secure, and full of promise than God's Word.

Most people don't get to hear God's voice audibly say, "I love you," every day. And even though we can read about His love all over the Bible, people's hearts rely too much on tangible experiences to determine their reality. Many times, trusting in God's unconditional love for us can feel so counterintuitive and so illogical.

This means that sometimes we have to lovingly lead our hearts to counterintuitively trust in the unseen more than the seen.

How do we get there with God?

Earlier, we learned how God is preparing the way for our Heart Logic to be rewritten. We recognized that our Sore Spots lose their influence as we let God's love, grace, and presence replace the old insecurity, fear, and pride in our hearts. Although we may still be tempted to lean into the familiar voice of Sore Spots at times, we gain the capacity through the healing process to put their deceptive voice back in their rightful place. That means we have found freedom from Sore Spots getting in the way in the present process of reevaluating the answers to the Heart Logic questions. We are primed to do the counterintuitive—to show our hearts that they can trust what God says to be true more than what's seen, felt, and lived.

To do that, we have to develop "double vision." We're not referring to the bad kind of double vision that is a symptom of a serious health condition, but the spiritual double vision that sees both our circumstances and God's promises simultaneously.

We adopt double vision as we bring our experiences into relationship with the truth, even when both seem opposing to each other. Usually, we often try to just ignore one or the other because we don't know what to do with the apparent opposition.

Here's the problem with singular vision. Focusing on experience without acknowledging God's truth leaves us hopeless and helpless. Likewise, focusing on God's truth without acknowledging the experience leaves us in denial. Neither are good.

We must acknowledge both experience and truth and bring them into a relationship with each other to actually be living in faith. However, we do not put these two on an equal footing. We guide our heart beyond *what is seen into the unseen*. We show experience that it is valid, but there is a truth that prevails in spite of it.

Healthy double vision is careful to let God's promises redefine life, not life redefine God's promises. It allows us to free our hearts from the oppression of lived experiences and enjoy the peace, hope, and comfort that come from truth.

As we try to apply double vision to help us say "yes" to the Heart Logic questions, we'll need to reexamine the Heart Shapers in our life stories that have cast doubt on the goodness of God, ourselves, others, and life. Look at one of your Heart Shapers and ask yourself, *"What does God say about that experience that was true, that the experience itself couldn't show me?"*

What would happen to your heart's doubt in God's ultimate goodness if you could reimagine that moment with Him in it?

If it was a moment where you felt unprotected, perhaps having a bad car accident that wasn't your fault or being at the mercy of a raging parent, your intuition might have told you that God was not there. He didn't show up. He didn't protect you. You'll have trouble saying "yes" to the question, *"Is God good? Is He really good all the time?"*

What would happen to your heart's doubt about God's goodness if you could reimagine that moment with Him in it?

When you ask, *"Where was God?"* begin to imagine Him there with you, wrapping His arms around you and weeping over your pain (Psalm 56:8).

When you wrestle with this challenge, *"This didn't feel like protection from God,"* begin to acknowledge that His presence is protection. He stands with you beyond the pain to turn that pain into purpose (Romans 8:28).

When you can't reconcile why God would let that happen to you and not step in a bad situation, submit yourself to the truth. His purposes will never be fully understood by me or you. But, it's possible that He sees a bigger story being told than you could see (Proverbs 3:5-6).

> *God brings goodness into the pain, but maybe it just hasn't yet arrived in your circumstance.*

In order to get to your heart to say *"yes"* to any Heart Logic question you've struggled with, you'll have to step into the competition happening in your heart and adopt some double vision. Sometimes, we can even find tangible goodness in our circumstances if we open our eyes from their tunnel vision and look hard enough. Even when there seems to be no way to put the "goodness spin" on your divorce or child's crippling mental health issue, there's still evidence of God's goodness all around you. God brings goodness into the pain, but maybe it just hasn't yet arrived in your circumstance. We have to trust His Word to sustain us in those moments by casting our assessment of goodness far beyond the present moment.

How can we really be sure that we haven't just set ourselves up with some nice exercise of choosing blind optimism over reality? Sometimes we have to give God an opportunity to become a little *more seen.*

We may not physically see God or hear His audible voice, but we can absolutely give God the opportunity to show up and give our hearts the opportunity to experience Him. That helps make truth feel just a little more intuitive.

It might be a moment with scriptures that affirm the goodness of God, you, others, or life. He might use that time to press a word or phrase into your heart to affirm His truth.

It might be a moment of silence and solitude with God, where you ask Him to show you where He was when you were being assaulted. Perhaps you'll have a picture form in your mind that shows you God's heart.

It might be a moment of listening to worship music where you feel God stirring something in you through the words of the song.

None of the healing of your Heart Logic will happen without the power of the Holy Spirit. This cannot just be a cognitive exercise of rewriting your answers to some simple questions so you can *know* God differently. This is about *experiencing* God differently. Experience is active. It's personal. It's relational. Experiencing God differently requires you to get quiet with God, so He can be the one to convince your heart that it can trust His Word.

This is about experiencing God differently.

You might have to do some deeper healing work along the way to help your heart really receive "yes" answers to the Heart Logic questions to make these a reality in your heart, not just your head. You may need to heal from some trauma or work on reshaping your image of God. You'll likely need a counselor or coach to help you do that. You will most certainly need God most of all.

How will you answer the four Heart Logic questions? Will you take the opportunity to bring your heart into deeper alignment with God by erasing your doubts, caveats, and exceptions to one of the questions?

Let go of what makes sense to your misaligned heart.

You are called to the counterintuitive life with Jesus. Let go of what makes sense to your misaligned heart. Let go of those doubts fed by the seen and lived. Lean into God's truth. It is trustworthy.

Prayer:

God, help me to see you in everything. Show me the places where my intuitive perspective doesn't match how you would see it. I ask that you give me double vision to see that your truth and goodness have been with me all along. I desire to answer each Heart Logic question with a resounding, "Yes!" Amen.

Reflection Questions:

Notice the places you hesitate when you add a life experience on the end of a Heart Logic prompt.

God is good, but what about . . . ?

I am good, but how come . . . ?

People are good, but they . . . .

Life is good, except when . . . .

How does God want you to rethink those exceptions?

What does having double vision mean to you? Can you think of a time in your life when you had it? How did that impact your experience? Can you think of a time you needed it but didn't have it? How did that affect you?

What stood out to you most in today's reading?

Relying only on my life experiences and living in the seen means I may never fully be able to answer "yes" to the four Heart Logic questions. But I have a chance to revise my answers!

Security, Ruthless Trust, and Unshakable Hope

W hat's the big deal about being able to say "yes" to these four Heart Logic questions?

It's a big deal indeed! Aligning your Heart Logic with God's truth sets off a chain reaction of emotional and spiritual development that makes the difference between a life defined by *fighting for faith* or a life *led by faith*. I hope that has your attention.

I want to help you understand the chain reaction that Heart Logic induces within you so you can fully appreciate the power of getting your Heart Logic right.

Step One: Security
The power of saying "yes" to the Heart Logic questions begins by building a bedrock of security in you.

Think about it.

When your heart asks, *"Is God good?"* it is wondering if you're safe and secure with Him.

When your heart asks, *"Am I good?"* it is wondering if you can be secure in who you are.

When your heart asks, *"Are other people good?"* it is wondering whether it is safe to trust them.

Ruthless trust and unshakable hope can only be found in God.

When your heart asks, *"Is life good?"* it is wondering if God has a purpose even in the most difficult times.

Security is found in God and not in ourselves, our performance, people, or our circumstances.

Security simply means that you rest assured in every situation. Your instincts tell you that you are going to be okay no matter what. They tell you that God's got you and that you are safe.

I think Jesus was inviting us into a secure life with Him when He said, "Keep company with me and you'll learn to live freely and lightly" (Matthew 11:30, *MSG*).

Has your security been compromised by being unsure of one of the Heart Logic questions? You can get through life with compromised security, but you will pay the price by living hindered. Things such as nagging self-doubt, over-reliance on yourself instead of God, holding back too much from others, or living anxiously as you wait for the next thing to go wrong will all prove to hinder your heart.

Too often, we look for security in who we are by impressing people and accomplishing great things. With God, security comes from the profound understanding that He knows the worst about us and loves us still. Security is also found as we affirm the true character of God, which gives us the ability to courageously release control even when we cannot understand.

Security grows when we see enough good in humanity to begin to believe the best in someone. Security can also be found in the profound ability to see beyond the pain when our worst nightmares happen but still lean into the comfort of Jesus.

Step Two: Ruthless Trust and Unshakable Hope
Two things that you do not want to live life without become possible with security as the foundation in your heart. They are *trust* and *hope*. This is the kind of trust and hope that are not for the faint of heart. Ruthless trust and unshakable hope can only be found in God.

Ruthless means having no pity. Ruthless *trust* means having no pity or excuses for ourselves—even when we don't see the logic of what's being asked of us, or we see no way out.

Is your heart secure enough to trust others who are trustworthy, long before they have "proven" themselves by making it through your grueling gauntlet of trust

Trust is a remarkable thing.

tests? Does your heart feel safe enough with God to turn your palms up in the middle of a mystery and prayerfully say, "Your will be done"? Is your heart assured enough of who you are to step out of self-judgment and confidently step into using your gifts?

Brennan Manning, author of the book *Ruthless Trust,* said,

The reality of naked trust is the life of the pilgrim who leaves what is nailed down, obvious, and secure, and walks into the unknown without any rational explanation to justify the decision or guarantee the future. Why? Because God has signaled the movement and offered it his presence and his promise.[7]

May you also be compelled by more of Manning's words, "Trust is our gift back to God, and he finds it so enchanting that Jesus died for love of it."[8]

Trust is a remarkable thing. It gives you the gift of having something other than yourself to rely on. Trust makes you able to say "yes" to the Holy Spirit and do counterintuitive things for God.

Unshakable hope believes in God's good purposes even when we don't see them happening yet.

Unshakable means unable to be unchanged. Having unshakable hope means that you keep anticipating goodness even when circumstances give you no reason to expect anything good. Unshakable hope believes in God's good purposes even when we don't see them happening yet.

Just like ruthless trust, unshakable hope is a remarkable thing. It guards us from resignation and helplessness. It tends to the cries of agony in our hearts. It gives us the ability to believe in something greater than the pain or possibility of the present.

---

7   Brennan Manning, *Ruthless Trust: The Ragamuffin's Path to God* (New York: HarperCollins, 2010), 12-13.

8   Ibid, 2.

When circumstances are unkind and hope is not evident around us, we have to adopt double vision (Day 3) to keep our unshakable hope alive.

Abraham had double vision that brought him hope when it appeared hopeless. God asked Abraham to do something unthinkable. "Take your son, your only son, whom you love—Isaac—and go to the region of Moriah. Sacrifice him there as a burnt offering on a mountain I will show you" (Genesis 22:2). Abraham was obedient. Can you believe that? Most parents think, *I would never be able to do that, even if I heard God loud and clear!* But Abraham had something profound within him that made him able: ruthless trust and unshakable hope.

Hebrews 11:19a shows that hope was alive in him when it states, "Abraham reasoned that if Isaac died, God was able to bring him back to life again." His double vision allowed him to see that moment as hopeful because of the way the promises and power of God could redefine even death.

Is your heart secure enough to have double vision and do counterintuitive things for God? Do you feel assured enough to have the kind of hope that carries you through unrelenting trials?

Without ruthless trust and unshakable hope, something can only be as good as its circumstances, and we can only be as obedient as our logic allows. With them, we can step into a faith that makes us fully alive.

> With them, we can step into a faith that makes us fully alive.

Prayer:
_____

God, I desire to have my security solely in you, not myself, others, or circumstances. I desire to live my life with ruthless truth and unshakable hope. As I surrender my heart to you, help my faith to flourish like Abraham's. Amen.

Reflection Questions:
_____

Reflect on the statement, "Security simply means that you rest assured in every situation. Your instincts tell you that you are going to be okay no matter what. They tell you that God's got you and that you are safe." How does this resonate with your heart?

Would you say that you have ruthless trust and unshakable hope?

What stood out to you most in today's reading?

When our security becomes firm by being able to answer "yes" to the four Heart Logic questions, we can have ruthless trust and unshakable hope.

DAY 5:

Unhindered Faith

Yesterday, you saw the beginnings of the remarkable progression of emotional and spiritual development that your Heart Logic ignites. The "yes" answers build security that propels ruthless trust and unshakable hope in your heart (Steps One and Two).

What happens next? Ruthless trust and unshakable hope ignite deeper faith than you've ever known!

Step Three: Unhindered Faith
Martin Luther said, "Faith is a living, bold trust in God's grace, so certain of God's favor that it would risk death a thousand times trusting in it. Such confidence and knowledge of God's grace makes you happy, joyful and bold in your relationship to God and all creatures."[9]

---

9 Martin Luther's Definition of Faith: An excerpt from "An Introduction to St. Paul's Letter to the Romans," Luther's German Bible of 1522 by Martin Luther, 1483-1546. Translated by Rev. Robert E. Smith from DR. MARTIN LUTHER'S VERMISCHTE DEUTSCHE SCHRIFTEN. Johann K. Irmischer, ed. Vol. 63(Erlangen: Heyder and Zimmer, 1854), pp.124-125. [EA 63:124-125] August 1994.

The writer to the Hebrews affirms Luther's conviction: "Faith is the assurance of things you have hoped for, the absolute conviction that there are realities you've never seen" (Hebrews 11:1, Voice).

Here's the exciting conclusion these writings lead me to:

Ruthless trust + unshakable hope = unhindered faith.

When our hearts rest in security, trust, and hope, they come into alignment *with* God. This is where we move ourselves into an incredibly powerful position of having unhindered access to faith! This is the kind of faith described by Martin Luther.

Isn't that the goal most of us have been chasing since we decided to follow Jesus? We just want faith to come naturally. We don't want to have to work so hard to feel and do the things that faith expects.

Ruthless trust and unshakable hope ignite deeper faith than you've ever known!

For example, instead of forcing ourselves to accept whichever outcome God chooses to allow, we would much rather be able to just readily accept what He brings because we trust Him. Instead of just going about life hoping that it will turn out okay, we would much rather be able to live each day full of hope and excitement for what is to come.

We all desire to experience God by becoming so secure in His love and who that means we are: fully known, seen, and deeply loved.

I had the privilege of watching unhindered faith in action as my dad faced cancer in 2019.

I am incredibly thankful today to get to call him a cancer survivor. I'm also incredibly thankful to have witnessed his unhindered faith that made his battle with cancer as painless as possible (relatively of course!).

His faith wasn't hindered by fear.

Like many other tragedies and challenges that insert us into ambiguity and threat, cancer will reveal pretty quickly how deeply trust and hope are woven into the fabric of our faith.

The constant refrain through the couple of months from his diagnosis to surgery was, "I didn't see this one coming." Even after all the health challenges he'd been through before, cancer did not run in the family and wasn't an expected companion. In the time leading up to the surgery to try to remove the tumor, there were unknowns about how serious this battle with cancer would be. No one knew what they would find during surgery or whether it had spread.

He had the tall order of living through this ambiguous time without letting his mind go on a wild, fearful ride of made-up stories.

If they discover this is worse than they thought, it's not going to be okay.

If it's metastasized, then it's inevitable this will take my life.

I cannot deal with surgery one more time, after the four awful surgeries I've been through before.

If fear had control of his heart, he would have been in serious trouble. It would have left him obsessing about the what-ifs, dwelling on how awful the surgery will be, and grasping for unhealthy control through his old normal of over-researching and trying to be prepared with plans A through E. Fear would have smothered his trust and hope and left him defeated

He was secure; He knew that he could trust God.

before he began: anxious, desperate, and feeling unprotected.

But his faith wasn't hindered by fear. Instead, he had access to dynamic and unhindered faith built on an unwavering belief that God is good and that life is good, even when cancer is allowed into a faithful servant's life.

He was secure. He knew that he was going to be okay, whether it meant healing on this earth or an early ticket to eternity with Jesus.

He knew that he could trust God, even when he personally couldn't understand what was happening and couldn't fix it himself. He was convinced that God wouldn't do him harm either; so if cancer would be part of his future, he could accept that without changing his view of God as a good and loving Father.

He had hope beyond his circumstances. He was able to let his view of eternal life with God take the sting out of a potentially early exit from this life. He could hope in something that cancer couldn't take away.

A few days before the surgery, I remember him sending me a couple of recordings of songs that an old friend had made for him. They were anthems that reminded him to cling to his faith, to keep saying "Yes, God is good no matter what!"

The lyrics of one of the songs he played on repeat, "God Is So Good" written by Pat Barrett, read:

No height or depth can separate
Your steadfast love we can't escape
Your faithfulness, an endless sea
So full of grace and mercy
We sing
God is so good
God is so good
God is so good
He's so good to me

My dad was still human, so it wasn't as if he felt joyful and excited about cancer or major surgery. The first thoughts that came to my dad's mind once in a while might have been flavored by fear. But he made the choice to trust his second thought, the thought that was defined by his faith.

With ruthless trust and unshakable hope defining his heart, my dad showed up to that surgery with unhindered faith leading his way. He showed up to the surgery with a heavy dose of anticipation but not fear. He had a healthy awareness about what could go wrong, but he was not defeated. Trust and hope won.

He had hope beyond his circumstances.

The refrains of his heart were:

I have to face cancer, yet the Lord is with me.

I have hope long beyond this life and that there are worse things than dying.

I've been through plenty of difficult surgeries before; nevertheless, I trust that God will walk with me through this one too.

That's counterintuitive, isn't it? Relaxing, trusting, and yielding instead of getting uptight, afraid, and grasping for control. It goes against the normal to face ambiguity yet remain sure that God will be faithful. But counter-

Unhindered faith is not limited by wavering doubts.

intuitive approach, made possible by faith, made the process so much smoother. With unhindered faith, my dad may have been physically weak because of cancer, but he was spiritually and emotionally strong. That turned cancer from a feared enemy into a challenge he was ready to either overcome or endure.

Unhindered faith is not limited by wavering doubts. It's not tempered by exceptions we've made to what God says is true. It is utterly expectant. Unhindered faith means instinctually expecting God to show up as the God He says He is—present, loving, merciful and your pursuer, protector, peace, and guide.

Do you want to live a life of unhindered faith? Not mediocre faith, but dynamic and bold faith that allows you to live *with* Jesus. Do you want the kind of faith that makes your vision His vision? Do you want to make your ways His ways?

If your heart stays unaligned (even a little) with God's promises of goodness (faulty Heart Logic), you'll be left only longing for your faith to feel more like an instinct rather than a product of willpower. Your heart will constantly be fighting against your faith and making it harder than it should be to relax and rest in the love of God.

There's no way to get the kind of faith you want without unhindering your heart from all that's holding it back. The power of saying "yes" to these four little Heart Logic questions is real.

Aligning your heart with God's promises of His goodness, your goodness (because of Him), goodness in humanity, and life's goodness swings the door wide open to something that didn't exist in your life before.

It opens up the door just a little wider to a secure life where you rest in safety and assurance. It's a life where you get the gift of ruthless trust and unshakable hope to quiet the fear, shame, self-doubt, anxiety, helplessness, and despair that try to take over. It's a life where faith is dynamic and unhindered. That's the kind of faith where God isn't a piece of knowledge; He's an experience. The door is opened for an unhindered heart to set the trajectory for an unhindered life.

Doesn't that sound like freedom?

Prayer:

God, thank you for being good, present, loving, and merciful. I believe that you are my pursuer, protector, peace, and guide. I desire more than anything to rest in who you are and what that means for my life. I want unhindered faith! God, help me stand on the ruthless trust and unshakable hope that will create it. Amen.

Reflection Questions:

What piece of your story or question that you have keeps you from living with unhindered faith?

What excites you about the possibility of living with unhindered faith?

What stood out to you most in today's reading?

God desires for us to live with unhindered faith, full of trust and hope in who He is: good, present, loving, merciful, and our pursuer, protector, peace, and guide.

WEEK 3: GROUP QUESTIONS

1) Were you surprised at how you initially answered the four Heart Logic questions? If you feel comfortable, share the question you have struggled with the most.

2) Do you have any exceptions to your answers? (Is there a "But..." that your heart wants to add to the end of a Heart Logic question?)

3) What does having double vision (From Day 3's reading) mean to you? Think of a time in your life when you had it, and share how it impacted your experience. Think of a time you might have needed it but didn't have it.

4) Would you say that you have security, ruthless trust, and unshakable hope? What step is God asking you to take toward having them in your life?

5) Are your answers to the Heart Logic questions competing with your faith? What question, exception, or piece of your story keeps you from living with unhindered faith?

WEEK 4:

Private Conclusions & Life Outcomes

little "t" truth and small "s" strategies

The sower may mistake and sow his peas crookedly: the peas make no mistake, but come up and show his line.
—RALPH WALDO EMERSON

Just as the peas will show the sower's crooked lines, the contents of your mind will show what's sown crookedly in your heart.

Remember from week one: "Above all else, guard your heart for everything you do flows from it" (Proverbs 4:23).

The contents of our hearts and minds are not independent; they are both parts of core being. There's no separating them from one another. The heart of the matter is that the heart matters. Our hearts are the original curators of meaning and understanding that we described as Heart Logic. Over the last few weeks, we've seen the power of the heart to shape everything else that flows through us. It's no doubt that the foundational meanings made (Heart Logic) directly shape more developed thinking and strategizing we do in our daily lives.

It's also no surprise that the direct consequence of a hindered heart is a hindered mind. We either see the unhindered faith that our hearts can produce showing up in our minds, or we see the lack of it.

If our hearts are still overly influenced by Sore Spots and faulty Heart Logic, too often our minds will be ruled by our flesh (our old pain) more than our faith. When our hearts are hindered, we'll think through a lens of self-protection, pessimism, or control (like our old pain tells us to) instead of hope and trust like unhindered faith tells us to. Our behavior won't be evidence of our faith, either. Self-reliance, rage, wearing masks to hide our true selves, keeping relationships shallow, or self-medicating will be our misguided instincts.

Just as the peas will show the sower's crooked lines, the contents of your mind will show what's sown crookedly in your heart.

Remember, our minds will just fall in line with the directions the heart is giving them to avoid more pain and protect themselves.

There are two primary elements that our minds are responsible for—our thoughts (beliefs, interpretations, and lessons) and our strategies (choices, postures, and actions). Collectively, we call the personal patterns we develop in our thinking and strategies our *Private Conclusions*.

Your Private Conclusions are called "private" not because they're meant to be secret, but because they're hidden deep in your soul. Sometimes they're even private from you, meaning you don't even realize they're within you!

Your Private Conclusions will be made of two things that can depart from God's intentions: little "t" truth (your experiential truth) and small "s" strategies (your personal strategies).

Remember, our minds will just fall in line with the directions the heart is giving them to avoid more pain and protect themselves.

little "t" truth

The deepest meaning and understanding you carry (your Heart Logic) influence the more detailed and defined thinking you do as you go through daily life, which includes many *little "t" truths.*

Little "t" truth is our experiential truth. It's what appears true because we've seen it, lived it, or felt it. Not all little "t" truths are a problem. Sometimes you get lucky and what you experience in life matches God's perspective (Big "T" Truth). Too often, life experiences compete with the perspective of God, and our little "t" truths become sneakily influenced by old pain that's been trapped in our hearts. That's when our little "t" truths can become untrustworthy. Also, little "t" truths easily fool us into undeserved loyalty because they feel awfully true even when they aren't aligned with God.

Your mind progresses from the high-level Heart Logic questions you ask early in life like, *"Am I enough?"* to, *"Why doesn't my wife want to spend more time with me?"* As you draw more detailed conclusions in these moments, you establish little "t" truths. As you've learned, you can't always trust experience to be a wise teacher! Yet, little "t" truths are often treated as gospel before they are examined.

Our little "t" truths easily fool us into undeserved loyalty because they feel awfully true even when they aren't aligned with God.

If a car accident unfairly steals your son, and your Heart Logic tells you that God is good *most* of the time (but not *all* the time), your heart lies vulnerable. Your little "t" truth of the moment might be: *"I guess God isn't really a protector like He says if He didn't stop this accident from happening."* You might *want* to believe that God is in it, but you'll doubt too much for that to comfort you or keep you from resenting God.

If you are experiencing financial problems and are currently without a job, your Heart Logic may already say, *"Life isn't very good, especially when it's hard."* As you continue to struggle, your heart stands little chance against this little "t" truth. *"Life is so unfair that I shouldn't expect anything good to come."* You're headed for frustration, anger, disillusionment, and depression.

Here are a few other examples of little "t" truths:

- I shouldn't get too close to these new people because everyone ends up leaving at some point.

- Risk taking is always stupid! If you can't guarantee things will be okay, it's not smart to go forward.

- It's too selfish for me to slow down long enough to take care of myself. Other people need me too much.

Can you see the problem with these thoughts? (If you can't, pay attention!) Little "t" truths will steal life from you and leave you hindered. They affirm that you aren't secure, that it's wise not to trust, and that hope is for the naive. They keep you from seeing as God sees, and that's always a compromised perspective. Things will look bleaker to you than they should. You will doubt when there's no good reason to doubt. You'll risk misunderstanding others' hearts as darker than they really are.

small "s" strategies
This is a fact: Your choices always line up with what you believe to be true. Life strategies based on little "t" truths are called *small "s" strategies*.

Small "s" strategies are the things we do in order to try to be okay, given the distorted reality that a little "t" truth has created. Small "s" strategies that oppose God's intentions for how to live, love, and serve will end up hindering Life Outcomes like our relationships, character, peace, and joy.

Here are several examples of small "s" strategies that might make you feel better in the moment but lead you down a path of hindered living.

1) *Hide.* Be invisible or wear a mask.
2) *Deny.* Pretend nothing is wrong.
3) *Settle.* Accept that this is as good as it gets.
4) *Self-sufficiency.* Rely totally on yourself.
5) *Go numb.* Don't risk feeling the weight of reality.

6) *Compartmentalize.* Separate parts of your life or identity to deal with incongruence.
7) *Achieve.* Keep performing and winning to try to feel valuable.
8) *Control.* Keep everything under your influence.
9) *Stay busy.* Cover things up with activity.
10) *Indulge.* Quiet the discomfort with unhealthy ways of soothing.

Your small "s" strategies may be your ways of coping, feeling successful or safe, relating to others, engaging (or disengaging) with your emotions, and so much more.

Sometimes we justify the small "s" strategies so well that we aren't bothered by them (even though we should be). Other times we're exasperated by them, and we just don't know how to stop. In those cases, we find ourselves echoing the words of Paul when he said, "I do not understand what I do. For what I want to do I do not do, but what I hate I do" (Romans 7:15).

Our hindered hearts will have trouble getting beyond the allure of perceived safety in small "s" strategies. Sometimes we continue to do what's natural because its familiarity has numbed us to the dangers. Sometimes we've just stopped caring about the consequences.

This is a fact: Your choices always line up with what you believe to be true.

Many of your small "s" strategies were probably developed because they worked for you under certain circumstances, and you decided, *Why mess with a good thing?* But what once helped you survive often becomes the very thing that prevents you from thriving!

On the surface, many small "s" strategies don't sound bad—work harder, fix a problem, protect yourself. With the right motivation, under the right conditions, and done to a healthy degree, they're not wrong at all.

But when strategies are driven by a need to compensate for and cover up the old pain in our hearts, they're good things gone wrong.

What once helped you survive often becomes the very thing that prevents you from thriving!

Isaiah 55:8-9 (NLT) keeps us humble with these words,

> *"My thoughts are nothing like your thoughts," says the Lord. "And my ways are far beyond anything you could imagine. For just as the heavens are higher than the earth, so my ways are higher than your ways and my thoughts higher than your thoughts."*

When we're in the ruts of little "t" truths and small "s" strategies, the distance between our thoughts and ways and God's can seem like an uncrossable chasm.

It is true that we'll never think just like God. There's no way we could ever come close to understanding His eternal viewpoint. It is true that we'll never act just like God wants us to. We're human, of course.

But we can find greater alignment with God's thoughts and ways than our hindered hearts have allowed.

As we do the work to recognize our misalignment, we can grow and heal. Our hindered faith can finally begin to move toward a new way of operating and thinking; a way full of security, hope, and trust. This Big "T" way of thinking will help us show up as our true selves, love others more freely, lead the way with generosity, or maybe even pursue a God-sized dream.

We can find greater alignment with God's thoughts and ways than our hindered hearts have allowed.

God has invited you to unhinder your heart so you can enjoy its fruit—an unhindered mind that will allow you to see a little more of what God can see and do a little more of what He would prescribe, especially in the face of uncertainty, adversity, or challenge!

Prayer:

God, you say that my thoughts are not your thoughts. Reveal the little "t" truths that I've been blindly accepting in my life. Open my eyes to thoughts I've relied on that don't reflect your heart. Make me willing to let go of them and discover how you see things so much more clearly than I do.

God, you say that my ways are not your ways. Help me see the small "s" strategies I've had that have separated me from you. Make me courageous enough to let go of them and know that you have a better way for me. I trust that even though it won't feel as safe at first, it will produce so much more freedom, joy, and peace than I've ever known.

Reflection Questions:

What little "t" truths might be misguiding you? (See Appendix C for examples)

Can you recognize where your little "t" truths might have come from? Can you connect them to other hindrances in your heart (faulty Heart Logic, Sore Spots, Heart Shapers)?

What small "s" strategies do you think you might be operating in currently? (See Appendix C for examples)

What stood out to you most in today's reading?

If your heart is hindered, your mind will be hindered too.

DAY 2:

Big "T" Truth

*Stop imitating the ideals and opinions of the culture
around you, but be inwardly transformed by the Holy
Spirit through a total reformation of how you think.
This will empower you to discern God's will as you live
a beautiful life, satisfying and perfect in his eyes.*
—ROMANS 12:2 (TPT)

God doesn't want to fit into your worldview; He wants to *recreate* your worldview. As you begin to view your world through God's perspective—*Big "T" Truths*, you get to experience the freedom of living an unhindered life.

Truth by definition is singular, so there is only room for one voice of truth: God's. No exceptions! Jesus was very clear that He is the source of truth: "If you hold to my teaching, you are really my disciples. Then you will know the TRUTH and the TRUTH will set you free" (John 8:31b-32, emphasis added).

The process of transcendence depends on the simple but difficult process of trusting God's perspective more than our own. Solomon instructed us: "Trust in the Lord with all your heart and lean not on your own understanding; in all your ways submit to him, and he will make your paths straight" (Proverbs 3:5-6). Many of us don't just lean on our understanding—it's our crutch, our gurney, our ventilator!

You aren't at the mercy of your unwanted thoughts; you have the power to control them. Dr. Caroline Leaf explains that we have more power than we might think. As she discusses the process of protein synthesis, which is an essential component of memory formation, she writes,

God doesn't want to fit into your worldview; He wants to recreate your worldview.

Proteins are made and used to grow new branches to hold your thoughts, a process called protein synthesis. So, if we don't get rid of the thought, we reinforce it. This is quite phenomenal because science is confirming that we can choose to interfere with protein synthesis by our free will. If you say, "can't" or "won't," this is a decision of your free will and will actually cause protein synthesis and changes in the real estate of your brain. Now "bringing into captivity every thought" (2 Corinthians 10:5, KJV) starts to become a lot more important. Thoughts are constantly remodeled by the "renewing of your mind."[10]

God is calling you to pay more attention to His voice than the voice of past pain.

---

10 Dr. Caroline Leaf, *Who Switched Off My Brain: Controlling Toxic Thoughts and Emotions, Revised Edition* (Nashville: Thomas Nelson, 2009), 60.

Examples of Big "T" Truths:

- I don't need to have all the talents or intelligence because the Holy Spirit lives in me, making me better than I am. (2 Corinthians 12:9)

- God calls me precious and cares about every detail of my life. (Proverbs 3:15, Ephesians 2:10, Matthew 6:26)

- Following God's will and letting Him be in control means that I don't always have to anticipate and prepare for everything that might happen. (Proverbs 3:5-6)

- God knows all but I don't. He is the author of life, and I can submit with joy because I'm sure He knows far better than me. (Psalm 97:9, Revelation 22:13)

Does God's perspective hold ultimate authority in you? Even if you know God's perspective, can you really own it as yours? The battle begins with staking a claim over Big "T" Truths and allowing your heart to receive it more and more over time. However, it is not just a matter of hearing God's Word for the first time. Many already know God's perspective through and through, but the words have gotten stuck as information, failing to create transformation.

The process of transcendence depends on the simple but difficult process of trusting God's perspective more than our own.

We have to get beyond *The Two Gospels Syndrome*. We've become a victim of it when we believe one of God's Big "T" Truths (like *He is on your side* or *He will come through*) to be true for everyone but ourselves. Our logic and faith tell us it's true. But our life experience casts doubt and tells us this truth is too good to be true. We can often even preach it to others with conviction, but we still make ourselves the exception. That

You aren't at the mercy of your unwanted thoughts; you have the power to control them.

leaves us with two gospels: the true gospel and the one we've created for ourselves that has an exception or two made just for us.

You might have the Two Gospels Syndrome if you spent your life dealing with an impossible to please parent (your Heart Shaper) and that made the idea of God unconditionally loving you (Big "T" Truth) feel way too good to be true. Your head may believe in God's unconditional love, but your heart can't receive it. You may become so passionate about making sure everyone else knows just how much they can relax into God's love because you want them to have what you "can't" have.

If your story included a legalistic background that made everything about getting all the rules right in order to be enough (Heart Shaper), you might have the Two Gospels Syndrome too. You may be enslaved to constant self-criticism even though you're known for being incredibly generous with grace and permission to fail for others.

There's a big difference between *knowing* Big "T" Truth is true and *experiencing* it as true. If the Big "T" Truth is just words, it won't change you. You have to know that the Big "T" Truth is not just true, but that it's true for you.

You only get convinced in your heart when you've been able to experience it. Maybe this has been through a moment when Scripture has come alive and it feels like God is flashing the neon sign saying, "Pay attention! This is about you!" Maybe it has been a moment of encounter with God where something just clicks in your heart, or maybe it's the stirring of a phrase or a feeling inside of you that you just know is the Holy Spirit.

Jo Carr and Imogene Sorely capture the courage needed to take God's hand: "To leave the swaddling warmth of my cocoon, my status quo . . . I'm leery of heights Lord, even your heights."[11]

The fight is very real. We are up against a lifetime of experiential learning and the powerful force of pain. Powerful emotions are embedded in our little "t" truths, and they have been ingrained in our thoughts for decades! We don't know any other way to think, and going on without them feels too scary.

We have to get beyond the Two Gospels Syndrome.

As we face the daunting task of reorienting decades-long patterns of thinking, Dr. Leaf assures us, "Within four days you will feel the effects of changed thinking; within 21 days you will have built a whole new thought pattern, literally, a new circuit in your brain. Though brain change is immediate, the entire process takes time to complete."[12]

Prepare to fight the ongoing battle for your thoughts to become God's thoughts. As Max Lucado said, "God loves you just the way

---

11 Jo Carr and Imogene Sorely, *Plum Jelly and Stained Glass & Other Prayers* (Nashville: Abingdon Press, 1973), 7.

12 Leaf, *Who Switched Off My Brain . . .*

you are, but He *refuses* to leave you that way. He wants you to be just like Jesus."[13]

Prayer:

God, I desire your worldview and to see my life through your lens and perspective. More than anything I want your TRUTH to reign in my heart and in my life, so that I might experience the freedom, peace, and abundance you promise. Help me to work through the little "t" truths that I have believed, even unknowingly, and replace them with your TRUTH. Empower me through the Holy Spirit to experience these TRUTHS for myself. Amen.

13 Max Lucado, *Just Like Jesus: A Heart Like His* (Nashville: Thomas Nelson, 2012), 3.

Reflection Questions:

What have I believed with my head, and even shared as truth with others, that I might not believe in my heart?

What Big "T'" truths might God be inviting you to own as yours? (See Appendix D for examples)

What stood out to you most in today's reading?

God desires for me to do the hard work, so I can rest in His Big "T" Truths, not just with my head, but with my heart.

Big "S" Strategies

Don't just listen to the Word of Truth and not respond to it,
for that is the essence of self-deception. So always let his
Word become like poetry written and fulfilled by your life!
—JAMES 1:22 (TPT)

You've been shooting yourself in the foot. You've been voluntarily holding one hand behind your back. Whether on purpose or through unawareness, you've been sabotaging yourself.

How? By trusting the small "s" strategies to make things better.

Hiding may have helped me temporarily turn the volume down on the voice of shame inside me and let me pretend my alcohol problem wasn't as bad as it was. But it created even bigger problems than the shame (and shame always found a way to speak up again too). Here are some of the ripple effects of hiding:

- I only had myself to try to deal with problems like alcohol, and we're so much more likely to fall back into the old pattern or give up on our own.

- I wasn't letting most people really know all of me either, so I was wasting too much valuable energy managing images and being misunderstood.

- I even set myself up for my shame to be reinforced rather than removed. By trying to ignore my shame through hiding from others, it was left unchallenged and gained power.

Our old pain doesn't think Big "S" Strategies sound very smart sometimes, but we can trust that God is always on our side and know that His intentions for us are always for our good.

The irony is that finally facing others (especially my family) was curative because I experienced true grace. That was the only thing that would ever put my shame in its rightful place.

Once again, the intuitive (small "s" strategies) failed me. But the counterintuitive blessed me.

God has ways of living that He calls us to, called *Big "S" Strategies*. They deserve the capital "S" because they align with God's heart and Word and show us His intentions for how to live and love. Our old pain doesn't think Big "S" Strategies sound very smart sometimes, but we can trust that God is always on our side and know that His intentions for us are always for our good.

Here are a few of God's Big "S" Strategies:

1) *Live vulnerably.* Hold your head high and live openly and authentically in relationships with people you trust. (James 5:16, Galatians 6:2, 2 Timothy 2:15)

2) *Face reality.* Lean into "grace plus truth" to fully acknowledge your pain and struggles. (John 1:14, Psalm 34:17-18, Psalm 55:22, 1 Peter 5:7)

3) *Pursue discipleship.* Go beyond what's easy and known, and chase after God's purposes. (Hebrews 6:1, Hebrews 5:12-14, Luke 17:5, Isaiah 48:10)

4) *Depend.* Be more God-reliant than self-reliant and lean on trusted others. (Proverbs 3:5, Psalm 62:5-6, Proverbs 27:17, Galatians 6:2)

5) *Acknowledge and manage your feelings.* Experience life to the fullest. (John 10:10, Ecclesiastes 3:4, Romans 12:15, John 11:35)

6) *Integrate.* Assimilate all parts of your life into your awareness, identity, and self-image. (Proverbs 11:3, 1 John 1:9)

7) *Simply serve.* Rest in your God-given esteem so you can achieve as part of your service, not as a pursuit of personal success. (Colossians 3:23-24, John 7:24, Hebrews 11:6)

8) *Partner with God.* Let God be your leader, trusting that He is capable and good. (John 15:5, Colossians 1:17, 1 Chronicles 29:11-12, Jeremiah 10:23, Isaiah 30:21)

9) *Abide.* Slow down enough to be fully present in all situations. (Matthew 6:34, John 15:10, Psalm 16:11)

10) *Heal.* Let God heal the pain you've tried to cover up so you can be your true self. (2 Timothy 1:7, Psalm 34:18, 2 Kings 20:5)

When we walk through the healing process of transforming little "t" truths into Big "T" Truths, we're paving the way for Big "S" Strategies to follow. When you look through the lens of God's

Big "T" Truths, your small "s" strategies won't make sense to you anymore.

For example, if you've believed that you are only as valuable as your last performance (little "t" truth), it made sense for you to invest in trying to make everything perfect, even when that meant pushing far past the line of excellence or a job well done (small "s" strategy). But when you begin seeing your value as a static and stable result of God's incredible love (Big "T" Truth), perfectionism and striving no longer make sense. Why would you need to keep unnecessarily proving yourself through smashing another production goal when God has already approved of you, and He is the goal? (1 John 4:9, Isaiah 54:10)

When you look through the lens of God's Big "T" Truths, your small "s" strategies won't make sense to you anymore.

When you see yourself through the lens of secure love (Big "T" Truth), it makes sense to let go of impressing God and others to focus on being faithful *to* God (Big "S" Strategy). As the transition takes hold, you'll see a natural outflow of your new ways of thinking in your choices and actions. You don't have to memorize a long list of Big "S" Strategies to follow! You find yourself naturally doing things differently when your heart is more aligned with God.

In some cases, a new Big "S" Strategy will completely change the outcomes in your life. It will put you on a new trajectory and you'll see things change all around you. Perhaps as you abandon the strategy of frenetically accomplishing everything possible for doing only what God prompts you to accomplish, the team you lead will start feeling more valued and healthy alongside you.

Sometimes the changes we make are only visible in our inside world and don't vastly impact our outside world. Maybe the biggest impact of you abandoning the small "s" strategy of compartmentalization will be your self-awareness. But even so, don't underestimate the power of internal changes to create ripple effects that make us healthier like drawing us closer to God or freeing us from emotional weight.

With insight and courage, you can abandon small "s" strategies and trust that God's ways won't harm you. You will find life a lot easier when you boldly step into the unknown of Big "S" Strategies and give them a chance to lead you where you've always wanted to go. You will erase all the extra management you have to do, like constantly finding ways to numb pain and trying to fool people that you're "just fine." You just get to be you—your true self, unhindered.

Following God's path is life's greatest adventure. Begin to dream of what will be unlocked in your life by Big "T" Truths and Big "S" Strategies. Self-sabotaging won't be in your way. You'll get to untie your second hand from behind your back and see what you're capable of.

> With insight and courage, you can abandon small "s" strategies and trust that God's ways won't harm you.

Prayer:

God, as I surrender my small "s" strategies, I ask that you help me replace them with Big "S" Strategies. I desire to follow your path for my life. I desire to dream with you. I desire to abandon the old and begin anew with you leading my thoughts and heart. Give me wisdom, insight, and courage to do the work in my heart that you are calling me to do. Amen.

Reflection Questions:

Which Big "S" Strategy resonated with you most? (See Appendix E for examples)

What small "s" strategy needs to be replaced in your life with a Big "S" Strategy?

What stood out to you most in today's reading?

When we decide to walk in Big "T" Truths, the small "s" strategies we have (maybe even unknowingly) will not make sense anymore.

DAY 4:

Life Outcomes

Constantly be on your guard against phony prophets. They come disguised as lambs, appearing to be genuine, but on the inside they are like wild, ravenous wolves! You can spot them by their actions, for the fruits of their character will be obvious. You won't find sweet grapes hanging on a thorn bush, and you'll never pick good fruit from a tumbleweed. So if the tree is good, it will produce good fruit; but if the tree is bad, it will bear only rotten fruit and deserves to be cut down and burned. You'll know them by the obvious fruit of their lives and ministries.
—MATTHEW 7:15-20 (TPT)

What's in it for me? That's a good question to ask yourself when you're making a decision about a strategic partnership for your business or when your boss asks you to put in an extra twenty hours a week for a special project. You had better have a good answer to the question "why?" to make it worth it!

I wonder if you've even asked that question as you've been reading this book. It's natural for us to look for a payoff that makes an investment worth it.

Over the last couple of weeks, you've been presented with the chance to unhinder your heart to produce internal outcomes such as security, trust, hope, and faith. But those aren't very tangible outcomes are they? They might sound great or appear like things you are supposed to want. What you might really want are things that you can touch, feel, and wrap your arms around—like a better marriage, less depression, more joy, or freedom from a pornography problem. Let me assure you that you're on the right journey if that's what you want; the only way to lasting life change is through heart change. Let me also affirm that you *should* want those things! God wants them for you too! And finally, I urge you to consider that your heart is absolutely worth the investment and believe that you will receive a healthy return in all of those tangible areas.

An unhindered heart ultimately creates an unhindered life.

An unhindered life bears good fruit (Matthew 7:15-20). An unhindered life is free and light (Matthew 11:30, MSG), even when circumstances around you are not. An unhindered life impacts the world in ways that only you can. It even allows you to bring out the best in others.

God wants to see you unlocked from weight and baggage that's been unnecessarily impacting your life in several key areas:

1) *Your emotions.* Become full of things like joy, love, hope, peace, and contentment.

2) *Your relationships.* Experience things like companionship, ease, respect, and partnership in your relationships.

3) *Your spirituality.* Know God deeply, do life with God, surrender your will to God, and listen intently to God's voice.

4) *Your behavior.* Exercise self-control, honor yourself with soul care, and exemplify values like generosity, kindness, and loyalty.

5) *Your physical body.* Become free of stress-induced impacts like headaches, muscle tension, and gut problems; sleep peacefully; honor your body with care routines.

6) *Your character.* Show fruit of the spirit (Galatians 5:22-23) like patience, gentleness, and faithfulness; live with integrity and honor; put others before yourself.

Often, we get stuck in self-perpetuation loops that keep us headed for the same unwanted outcomes over and over again. The negative Life Outcomes we experience often end up reinforcing some of the hindrances within us. Isn't that maddening?

Your painful outcomes falsely confirm that the pain of your Sore

Often we get stuck in self-perpetuation loops that keep us headed for the same unwanted outcomes, over and over again.

Spot is irredeemable, and they may affirm your faulty Heart Logic, little "t" truths, and small "s" strategies. So, you keep doing what you've been doing because you're more convinced than ever that it's the right or the inevitable thing to do!

For example, Javon's career wasn't thriving (Life Outcome), and that disappointment convinced him that the inadequacy (Sore Spot) he'd always felt was on point! But it was the paralysis from his Sore Spot that created that outcome, not a reality that he was inadequate. Here's what happened. Javon was lacking confidence that he had what it takes to succeed (little "t" truth) so he ended up playing it too safe (his small "s" strategy). After getting looked over by his boss because of that, Javon was annoyed by not having a real seat at the decision-making table. Without the Sore Spot getting in his way, Javon could have been a contributor—he was smart enough and actually had a hundred ideas that his inadequacy was just keeping silenced. But now this disappointment in his career (Life Outcome), deepened his Sore Spot of inadequacy more than ever and fueled its continued influence, leaving him stuck in a self-perpetuating and devastating loop.

Until you unhinder your heart, you'll be stuck in a loop.

Until you unhinder your heart, you'll be stuck in a loop. You'll become more and more convinced that your little "t" truths are true and that small "s" strategies are the only thing that will work! Until something breaks the cycle, it plays on repeat.

So, what will break the cycle and set you on a new trajectory?

You can't change things from the outside in. A new routine won't ultimately fix your dread. More date nights won't ultimately fix the resentment in your marriage. Only a changed heart will. Hebrews 12:11 (NLT) promises those who partner with God in His training process will have a "peaceful harvest of right living for those who are trained in this way."

You can't change things from the outside in.

Do you want to actually know what it feels like for Jesus' words to be true of your life: "Keep company with me and you'll learn to live freely and lightly" (Matthew 11:30, MSG)? If you follow the pathway to unhinder your heart, your life will be unhindered too.

As you fix your eyes on what's in it for you, I hope a light has turned on inside of you. I hope you see a real pathway to get the result you've always wanted but gave up on because you didn't know how to get there.

It's more within your reach than ever.

Prayer:

God, I fix my eyes on you as I make changes to my heart and mind. I see the freedom on the other side of the hard work of learning about my heart. God help me imagine what my life can begin to look like if I unhinder my heart. Help me to partner with you as you lead me through this training process that will bring more health and contentment into my life. I believe that you will receive glory from this work and that it will all be for my good. Amen.

Reflection Questions:

How have the six Life Outcomes been impacted by the ways your heart has been hindered (by Sore Spots, small "s" strategies, etc.)? (See Appendix F for examples)

Emotional:

Relational:

Spiritual:

Physical:

Behavior:

Character:

What more do you want for yourself in each of the six Life Outcomes? (See Appendix F for examples)

Emotional:

Relational:

Spiritual:

Physical:

Behavior:

Character:

What stood out to you most in today's reading?

An unhindered heart ultimately creates an unhindered life.

Strength to Overcome, Endure, and Love

"If your soul is healthy, no external circumstance can destroy your life. If your soul is unhealthy, no external circumstance can redeem your life," states John Ortberg quoting Dallas Willard.[14]

Aligned Heart:

God-Inspired
Security
∨
Ruthless Trust
∨
Unshakable Hope
∨
Deep Faith
∨
Strength

14 John Ortberg, *Soul Keeping* (Grand Rapids: Zondervan, 2014), 40.

Beyond all the Life Outcomes you've been able to see so far, there's still something else in it for you. It's the pinnacle of this progressive development taking place inside of you. It's the ultimate difference maker between emotional and spiritual weakness and wellness.

What is it? It is strength—but not the kind of strength you might expect.

Samson, one of the last judges to rule over Israel before the kings, was renowned for his physical prowess (Judges 14-16). With his superhuman strength and unmatched muscle, he rivaled Superman or Hercules. He used his strength to kill a lion with his bare hands (Judges 14:6) and strike down a thousand men with the jawbone of a donkey (Judges 15:14-15).

Samson is remembered for his strength to endure and overcome the challenges before him, so he could accomplish God's purposes.

It wasn't his physical strength that earned him a mention in Hebrews 11, a chapter that recounts the stories of many heroes of the faith. Samson is remembered for his strength to endure and overcome the challenges before him, so he could accomplish God's purposes. That strength is really what made him a hero.

Actually, Samson's physical strength failed him. After falling in love with Delilah, she betrayed him to the Philistines by arranging for his hair to be cut (which departed him from obedience to the Lord as in Numbers 6:5).

After putting him to sleep on her lap, she called for someone to shave off the seven braids of his hair, and so began to subdue him. And his strength left him. Then she called, "Samson, the Philistines are upon you! He awoke from his sleep and thought, "I'll go out as before and shake myself free." But he did not know that the Lord had left him. Then the Philistines seized him, gouged out his eyes and took him down to Gaza. Binding him with bronze shackles, they set him to grinding grain in the prison.
—Judges 16:19-21

His loss of strength wasn't just about a haircut. The crux of the problem was that he was missing strength in his heart. Judges 16:20 says that "the Lord left him." Without his heart aligned with God, he was weak and vulnerable in every way to the attacks and suffering before him. In the end, Samson finds strength again.

Then Samson prayed to the Lord, "Sovereign Lord, remember me. Please, God, strengthen me just once more, and let me with one blow get revenge on the Philistines for my two eyes." Then Samson reached toward the two central pillars on which the temple stood. Bracing himself against them, his right hand on the one and his left hand on the other, Samson said, "Let me die with the Philistines!" Then he pushed with all his might, and down came the temple on the rulers and all the people in it. Thus he killed many more when he died than while he lived. —Judges 16:28-30

Yes, Samson's physical strength is returned to him to knock down the pillars and send the Philistines to their deaths, but

The crux of the problem was that he was missing strength in his heart.

the only reason he regained his physical strength was because he realigned his heart with God. He prayed for God to remember him (Judges 16:28) and through reigniting his faith, he was given strength to overcome and endure for God. He was captured, blinded, and enslaved. Nevertheless, he was resolved and emboldened to do what had to be done for God, even when it meant sacrificing his own life.

Physical strength can only take us so far, but emotional and spiritual strength made possible by faith cannot be defeated. Emotional and spiritual strength mean being so aligned with God that the per-

Physical strength can only take us so far, but emotional and spiritual strength made possible by faith cannot be defeated.

spectives of faith like trust and hope carry you when your own logic and ability to fix it fail you. Emotional and spiritual strength show up in two key ways:

1)   Strength to overcome or endure a challenge.

Just like Samson, we need to be able to endure suffering that doesn't end and overcome the challenges before us that we know can't be mastered in our own ability. Samson is just one of the heroes of the faith named in Hebrews 11 who did such things. He's in good company along with others like Noah, Abraham, and Sarah who are remembered for their strength to overcome and endure. As we began to see in week one's look at Hebrews 11, some had strength to overcome a challenge. "By faith these people overthrew kingdoms, ruled with justice, and received what

God had promised them" (Hebrews 11:33). Others had strength to endure a challenge that didn't end. "Some died by stoning, some were sawed in half, and others were killed with the sword" (Hebrews 11:37).

Sometimes there are speed bumps on the road that we have to overcome to get to a smoother path. We need to work through the gaping disconnect in our marriage instead of giving into the desire to just move on. We need to get through the threatening divides happening in our church over the new vision. We need to deal with the painful backlash happening over a leadership transition. We need to get through a very challenging season of parenting. We have to make it through the persecution, poverty, or abusive relationship that we feel we may never escape. We need strength to overcome.

Sometimes the road stays bumpy, and we have to stay the course through the constant jarring of the uneven ground beneath us that does not smooth out. We have to endure a lifelong chronic illness that steals our energy, constantly irritates, and leaves us misunderstood. We have to find a way to sustain through the continual onslaught of life events that fire like an automatic weapon. We have to live with the grief that will last forever after an untimely loss. We have to figure out a way to do life without a

We need the emotional and spiritual resources to untether our wellness from our circumstances and be okay when things around us are not okay.

friendship that has ultimately dissolved. We absolutely need strength to endure.

We need the emotional and spiritual resources to untether our wellness from our circumstances and be okay when things around us are not okay. For the heroes of the faith in Hebrews 11, emotional and spiritual strength didn't originate in their grit. It was birthed by their faith. So, it must be for us too.

2)   Strength to love and rest in love

Abraham was another hero of the faith remembered in Hebrews 11. Abraham loved so deeply. He loved God. He knew he was loved by God, and he loved others the way God loved him.

Earlier, we visited a piece of Abraham's story in Genesis 22 where he was asked by God to sacrifice his son, Isaac, on the altar even though God eventually spared him from following through with the ultimate action. The kind of love that's born from unhindered faith shows up in that story.

Abraham loved God so much that he chose radical obedience, even when that meant giving up his very own son. He knew he was loved by God so much that he resisted the temptation to label God's plan as unloving, even before he knew that it would end with a ram being sacrificed instead of Isaac (Genesis 2:12-14). Abraham even loved his son so much that he would not withhold him from being a part of the obedience story with God. He knew Isaac was loved by God too, and so he entrusted him to God fully and completely, in a way most parents could not fathom.

We all need strength to love.

Sometimes we need strength to love those who feel unlovable. We need to forgive the betrayer who is not sorry and does not even get it. Sometimes we have to respect the intrusive family member who manipulates, knows no boundaries, and judges at every opportunity. And maybe at times, we need the strength to love ourselves when we are disappointed with our own behavior and feel unlovable.

Sometimes we need strength to rest in the love God has for us when the world around us feels so unkind. When people's brokenness keeps them from telling you how much you matter and causes them to reject and overlook, you need the warmth of God's unconditional love to sustain you.

Sometimes we need strength to love God when His ways are so mysterious that our instincts want to put some distance between us and Him. Our faith needs to guide us back to embracing Him and trusting that He is always for us.

Strength to love and rest in love came from Abraham's faith. So must it for us too.

Most of us don't need superhuman strength to do what God has called us to do. But we do need emotional and spiritual strength to live the obedient, faithful,

> Most of us don't need superhuman strength to do what God has called us to do. But we do need emotional and spiritual strength to live the obedient, faithful, and counterintuitive life that God calls us to — the unhindered life.

and counterintuitive life that God calls us to—the unhindered life.

With a hindrance in us that is holding us back from fully believing the truth of God in our heart, not just our head, we've lost our strength. We don't have access to our faith the way we need to persevere, overcome, or love.

Our faith becomes strength that helps us overcome, endure, and love.

We often assume that our faith will be a source of strength when things get tough. *"Of course I trust God." "Of course I have hope that He's going to come through for me."* Sometimes we believe it, but our capacity for it has only been tested as far as life has been tough—and for some of us, it just hasn't been, yet. We naturally didn't expect that a hindrance was even there, so we just didn't know there'd be a cap to our faith.

We need to ensure that every little piece that makes up the foundations of our souls are aligned with God. We need to get fear out of the way so we actually trust God with our hearts the way we speak trust out of our mouths. We need to get pride off its throne so we can live surrendered to Jesus, not just preach surrender to others. With our Sore Spots' influence squelched, our hearts are ignited in their faith through building their foundation of security, trust, hope, and faith. As a result, we become emotionally and spiritually strong. Our faith becomes strength that helps us overcome, endure, and love.

That's a life of obedience to God.

One day, do you long to hear God say, "Well done, good and faithful servant." (Matthew 25:21)?

Prayer:

God, as I journey through this life, I long to have strength that only you can give. I recognize through the lives of Abraham and Samson that this is not a type of strength I can give myself. I ask that as I do the hard work of looking at my heart, answering hard questions, growing in trust and hope, and developing an unhindered faith, that you would strengthen every fiber of my being for the life you see ahead of me. I long to hear those words from you, "Well done, good and faithful servant." Amen.

Reflection Questions:

Have you valued emotional and spiritual strength as much as physical strength in your life?

What importance do emotional and spiritual strength play in your overall well-being?

Have you ever come to a place or event in your life that made you realize there was a cap on your faith? What did you learn in that event about your strength to overcome, endure, and love?

What stood out to you most in today's reading?

My faith gives me strength to overcome, endure, and love.

WEEK 4: GROUP QUESTIONS

1) What little "t" truths might be misguiding you? What Big "T" Truths is God inviting you to own as yours?

2) What small "s" strategies do you think you might be operating in currently? Which Big "S" Strategies resonated with you most?

3) What have been some of your Life Outcomes from living with a hindered heart? (See examples in Appendix F)

4) What changes would you like to see for yourself in each of the six Life Outcomes? (See examples in Appendix F)

5) Have you valued emotional and spiritual strength as much as physical strength in the past? How would your life be impacted by placing a higher priority on emotional and spiritual strength?

WEEK 5:

Fighting the Battle

DAY 1:

Fight for Your Heart

The quickest way for anyone to reach the sun and the light of day is not to run west, chasing after the setting sun, but to head east, plunging into the darkness until one comes to the sunrise.
—GERALD LAWSON SITTSER[15]

Eugene Peterson wrote a wonderful book about the power of discipline and tenacity called *A Long Obedience in the Same Direction*. The problem that I hope has surfaced for you is that you don't want to go in the same direction any longer! You need a new direction. Whether you're making a 180-degree turn or a 45-degree turn, a new trajectory will take you to an unhindered life. Your new direction is a better direction because it's God's direction.

You have to be ready to stay the course. You're going to be taking on a series of battles that must be fought on behalf of your soul.

---

15 Gerald Lawson Sittser, *A Grace Disguised: How the Soul Grows Through Loss* (Grand Rapids: Zondervan, 2004), 3.

Are you ready to fight long and fight hard? No war is won in a moment. One decisive battle is not responsible for ultimate victory, even if that's what receives the glory in history books. War is won through a series of battles whose triumphs accumulate to collectively weaken the enemy and push back its territory.

Your new direction is a better direction because it's God's direction.

You will be fighting ongoing battles to find your internal victory. You are fighting for your new normal, an unhindered life made possible by an unhindered heart. God will equip you with the weapons you need for the fight—His help, His Word, Godly community to support you, and the Holy Spirit within you. But you have to show up to fight.

Most people want quick and easy results without doing any of the hard work required for victory. It's a disease of our world today.

Some people even come to our intensive counseling weeks at Blessing Ranch Ministries with wishful thinking that if they work hard on their hearts for five days, they won't have to do any more hard work when they get home. That group of people is set up to fall right back into their old normal as soon as the momentum wears off. What a wasted opportunity! When it comes to your heart, don't stop one step short. God never does.

Purposefully, healing and growth is rarely instantaneous.

It probably won't be one lightbulb moment that changes everything. It will be a series of moments that compel you to surrender your old normal and embrace the new normal more and more over time.

It's doubtful that one encounter with God will erase every untrustworthy intuition you have. It will take many moments of remembering the authority of what He has said to you that finally makes it stick in your heart, not just your head.

It most likely won't be one therapy session that removes all of your trauma triggers. It will be a progressive healing that frees you from your fear and mistrust, as your heart learns to relax.

Alan Ahlgrim says, "Heart work is hard work."[16] God is calling you to fight for your heart, and He has a good reason for that. He knows this will take tenacity and the hard work of entering your pain, overcoming the barriers between your head and your heart, and taking the power back that you've given away. Remember from week one that God often and intentionally invites us into process healing (as opposed to miraculous healing) with Him. These opportunities exercise our faith muscles and particularly strengthen our trust and dependence.

Don't give in to that voice inside right now that says, *"I don't have time for this or I'm too tired for this."* No matter the time, energy, pain, and heartache, I promise that it's worth it. What is even better is that God promises it's worth it too!

Most people want quick and easy results without doing any of the hard work required for victory. It's a disease of our world today.

---

16 Alan Ahlgrim, "Tourist or Pilgrim." www.east91st.org/blog/tourist-or-pilgrim/.

Many of these ongoing battles that you will fight are incited by collisions. Collisions are the hundreds of moments when your old normal and new normal collide. You've been going along your way, gaining confidence in your growth, and then suddenly that voice of little "t" truth is so loud again. Without knowing what happened, every fiber in your body wants so desperately to lash out, run, cover up, blame everyone else, or justify it away (small "s" strategies). Your old normal is trying to entice you back into its grips.

In these moments of collision, it's critical that you protect the work God has already done in you and lead your soul into a deeper embrace of God's new truths and strategies for you.

A collision might be a moment you get triggered by something that reminds your heart of its old pain. Maybe it's a moment where your boss says something that feels a little intense, and you notice yourself having such a strong emotional reaction. You're triggered because this reminds you too much of your ex-husband's verbal abuse that

> When it comes to your heart, don't stop one step short. God never does.

you endured for decades. This is not just about your boss. This is about you too. It has fanned the flames of a little "t" truth inside of you: *"Any intensity is dangerous. You'd better shut it down."* It's tempting you with a self-protective small "s" strategy: run away. You are already planning how you'll quit your job and get out of there before this gets worse.

This is a moment to face a collision in your heart. Will you reactively protect yourself through quitting or even powering up against your boss? Or will you manage your own heart and gently remind it that it's okay and also that your boss isn't your ex-husband? That doesn't mean it's okay for your boss to be out of line. It just means that you need to manage your heart so you can see clearly and act wisely.

Purposefully, healing and growth are rarely instantaneous.

You have a choice to make in these moments of collision. Will you step back into the comfort of the old normal that will steal life, or will you choose the discomfort of the new normal that can actually bring life?

How you navigate these collisions will be the difference between sustained growth and a short-lived high. You've got to show up with the right attitude, ready to embrace collisions as opportunities for growth, not threats, so they can produce your next level of healing and growth. In these moments, trust that what God has done in you is real. If it is real, that means you can take control, reset, and reclaim the truth that belongs to you.

Take control when a collision happens and reset your heart:

1) *Stop.* Interrupt yourself from leaning into the allure of the familiar in a moment of collision. Say "no" to the old normal of little "t" truths and small "s" strategies.

2) *Think.* Let God remind you of the specific Big "T" Truth He's given you to quiet a triggered Sore Spot. Find a short phrase that captures your Truth that you can repeat and rehearse in this moment. Remember how personal the Truth is and how there's no way you're the exception. Stick with it as long as it takes to get your heart convinced and reset.

3) *Pray.* Invite God into that moment of collision with you. This isn't a cognitive battle. This is a spiritual battle. You need Him in it with you. Say "yes" to your new normal with God.

The battle isn't over when you have an "aha moment." The battle doesn't end with an intention to live unhindered. You're signing up for a long obedience in a new direction. Cumulatively, the ground you take each time you battle for your heart will add up to unhindering your life.

Alan Ahlgrim says, "Heart work is hard work."

Prayer:

God, give me a warrior's spirit. I pray for grit when I need it. I ask for an extra dose of patience along the way. I pray for resolve to keep going when I grow weary.

God, I want to embrace a long obedience in a new direction. Please be my compass that sets my course and redirects me as I need. Help me listen to your voice over my own and lean into you for strength and direction each time I encounter a collision. I trust your direction, and I know that you are for me.

Thank you for the ways you equip me for the battles ahead of me. Thank you for always being by my side, ready to encourage me and help me. Partnering with you in the battle is the greatest privilege. Amen.

Reflection Questions:

When might you expect to encounter collisions between your old normal and your new normal? In other words, what might trigger your old feelings and memories, causing you to lose momentary control?

How can you be prepared for the moments of battle so you are ready to take control of them?

What stood out to you most in today's reading?

Be ready to fight a series of ongoing battles for your heart with victories that will accumulate to push back the enemy (your hindrances) and lead you into unhindered living.

DAY 2:

Run to the Roar

In his book, *Through the Eyes of a Lion*, Levi Lusko unpacks lions' genius-hunting methodology that gets their prey to run right into their trap. Here is what they do. Female lions wait behind the prey for ambush while the male lions circle in front of the prey and let out their famous, panic-inducing roar. This leads the prey right into the true threat—the claws of the female lions who have been lying in wait.

Levi Lusko said,

> *Going with their guts causes them to make the last mistake of their short, little lives. It's counterintuitive, but the right choice would be to override their emotions and run toward the roar.*[17]

What does running into the roar mean for us? Fighting the battle. It's a call to face our pain, our fears, and our gut punches full on so that we can heal through them instead of trying to escape them through avoidance and denial. Escapism only lets things

---

17 Levi Lusko, *Through the Eyes of a Lion* (Nashville: Thomas Nelson, 2015).

accumulate in us and gives them a license to leak out of us at the most inopportune times.

Davey Blackburn, a pastor whose wife was tragically murdered in their home in 2015, wrote about how he decided to run into the roar by going right back to the spot he found his wife dead:

> As much as I didn't want to step back into that living room where I found her, I knew I couldn't keep that boxed up. The morning I returned, I put worship music in my earbuds, laid down in the spot I found her, wept, prayed and worshipped. And I'll tell you, something miraculous happened. After about 45 minutes of running toward the roar, and I was better. I had released it all. The darkness that, in my mind, had hovered over that location was now taken captive by a risen savior and I wasn't afraid of it anymore. Initially when you run toward the roar it's excruciating; but eventually it's healing.[18]

Escapism only lets things accumulate in us and gives them a license to leak out of us at the most inopportune times.

Can you imagine stepping into that scene? What must he have felt when he saw the house come into view as he rounded the corner onto that familiar street? What memories must have flooded him as he stepped through the door of the house, just the way he did that morning he found her body? What grief must have overtaken his heart as he fixed his eyes on that spot that felt the

---

18 Davey Blackburn, "Run toward the Roar," *Davey Blackburn*, Davey Blackburn (August 13, 2019): www.daveyblackburn.com/blog/run-toward-the-roar.

last warmth of her body? His heart must have been pushed to the max that day, but Davey didn't shy away from the pain. He ran into the roar and showed his heart that it was capable of not only making it through the onslaught of emotion, but of actually healing through it.

Running into the roar means a couple of key things for us. First, running into the roar means facing an initial moment of intensity by getting honest with ourselves about the thing we've been avoiding. Maybe it's how lonely our spouse is despite being in the same bed every night. It can be that our rigid eating routines are actually an eating disorder. We may need to face the wounding we're doing to the people around us with the intensity we do everything with.

Running into the roar means abandoning the temptation to make it everyone else's problem and actually get curious about what's in our hearts that is responsible for what we see coming out of us. Running into the roar means facing the hurt we've caused others and owning it with humility and empathy.

Second, running into the roar means embracing the repeated collisions (which you read about yesterday) that will happen between your old normal and your new normal. What you really need to understand at this point of the journey is that running into the roar isn't a one-time event. It's a

What you really need to understand at this point of the journey is that running into the roar isn't a one-time event. It's a constant companion on a healing journey.

constant companion on a healing journey.

Always remember who the enemy is that you're fighting. It's not yourself nor the regret of a decision you made. It's not your parent who wounded you. It's not your spouse or friend who left. It's not your boss who seems against you. The blame, anger, and torturous what-ifs that follow those focuses will leave you fighting the wrong battles and missing the true roar that's calling you. Your true enemies, in the battle for your heart, are *complacency* and a*voidance*. Keep that perspective straight to energize and motivate you to continually be ready to say, "I'm ready to run to the roar."

Your true enemies, in the battle for your heart, are complacency and avoidance.

An unhindered life waits for you when you repeatedly run to the roar.

Prayer:

God, please help me run into the roar every time! Please keep my ears tuned in to hear the roars and not grow complacent. Give me courage to do the counterintuitive in that moment. I know you'll meet me there! You are a God of comfort and care. You will show up to turn my mourning into joy or my ashes into beauty (Isaiah 61:3). God, I want to put your glory on display by showing what you can do when our pain or the stubbornness of our old ways are surrendered to you. Thank you for your never-ending love and care. Amen.

Reflection Questions:

What is the roar in your life that you've been avoiding?

What can motivate you to run into the roar?

What stood out to you most in today's reading?

Running to the roar,
the uncomfortable,
painful parts of our
story, is what ultimately
unhinders our hearts.

DAY 3:

The Nevertheless Principle

And that about wraps it up. God is strong, and he wants you strong. So take everything the Master has set out for you, well-made weapons of the best materials. And put them to use so you will be able to stand up to everything the Devil throws your way. This is no afternoon athletic contest that we'll walk away from and forget about in a couple of hours. This is for keeps, a life-or-death fight to the finish against the Devil and all his angels.
—EPHESIANS 6:10-12 (MSG)

What good is a gardener without sharp shears and a spade?

What good is a lawyer without a killer defense?

What good is a soldier on the front lines without a ready weapon?

What good is your insight if you aren't equipped with the tools to help it change you?

You've got to be equipped with the right tools to effectively battle for your heart.

Don't worry! God's in this with you, and He will equip you with everything you need. In Ephesians 6:13-18 (MSG), God says,

> *Be prepared. You're up against far more than you can handle on your own. Take all the help you can get, every weapon God has issued, so that when it's all over but the shouting you'll still be on your feet. Truth, righteousness, peace, faith, and salvation are more than words. Learn how to apply them. You'll need them throughout your life. God's Word is an indispensable weapon. In the same way, prayer is essential in this ongoing warfare. Pray hard and long. Pray for your brothers and sisters. Keep your eyes open. Keep each other's spirits up so that no one falls behind or drops out.*

Don't worry; God's in this with you, and He will equip you with everything you need.

He offers you two key things in this passage as weapons for the battles before you.

First, prayer *is essential in this ongoing warfare.* Don't ever forget this is a spiritual battle you are fighting. You need to bring God into this with you and use prayer as a powerful tool to defeat the opposition.

This passage also said that "God's Word is an indispensable weapon." You've got to know how to use God's Word well—as a tool that can lead you out of anxiety, self-condemnation, or helplessness and into the comfort and security of truth. You've been challenged over the last few weeks to realize that this isn't a matter of having *information* about what God says. This is a matter of letting transformation happen *because* of what God says.

Transformation only happens when His Word comes alive to our hearts. So let me equip you with a tool today that can help God's Word come alive when you need it the most.

The Nevertheless Principle

Earlier, you learned about stepping out of experiential little "t" truths (what you have learned to be true through experiences in life) and into counterintuitive Big "T" Truths (what God says about you and your experiences).

You also became aware of how Big "T" Truths ultimately lead you into Big "S" Strategies (how you live out that Truth), and how together they ultimately shape your Life Outcomes.

It's critical that you don't just lean into Big "T" Truth when you're at church on Sunday and inspired by great worship or when life is smooth and nothing is challenging. If you really want to live unhindered, you'll have to find a way to bring your heart and mind into submission to truth in the hard moments, even when your circumstance makes you feel that maybe your Big "T" Truth is too good to be true.

This is a matter of letting transformation happen because of what God says.

In these moments of battle, the tool you need is *The Nevertheless Principle*.

Transformation only happens when His Word comes alive to our hearts.

The Nevertheless Principle provides a way of reconciling a difficult reality to God's Word when they don't appear to fit together. To use it, we create statements that acknowledge our experience, feeling, or circumstance, yet guide our perspective into a more powerful truth that overrides it.

We can rely on one simple word to help our hearts trade our little "t" truths for Big "T" Truth: *nevertheless*.

The Nevertheless Principle sounds like this:

- "It feels like I can't do anything right and someone is always disappointed in me; nevertheless, I am enough because I am faithful to what God asks of me, and He smiles upon that, not my perfect performance." (John 15:15-16, Romans 5:8, Ephesians 2:8-9)

- "My dad is absent, unsupportive, and unpredictable; nevertheless, God is present, in pursuit, and His love is constant." (John 3:16, Romans 8:38)

- "My pastor just got found out in an affair and this feels cruel after all we've been through as a church; nevertheless, God creates purpose in every pain, and He will use this as training grounds for our hearts." (Romans 8:28, Hebrews 12:11)

- "God didn't bring justice the way I wanted Him to; nevertheless, God cares about this more than I do." (Psalm 46:10, Psalm 32:8, Isaiah 46:4)

- "I have messed up so badly and I feel like a screw-up; nevertheless, I'm still valued because of God's sufficient grace." (2 Corinthians 3:5, 2 Corinthians 12:9, 2 Corinthians 12:10)

- "My trust was broken multiple times by people I thought had my back; nevertheless, God will never fail me." (Deuteronomy 7:9, Joshua 21:45)

In order for this to mean something to your heart, you can't substitute *"and"* for nevertheless.

"And" means both sides carry equal weight. "Nevertheless" is a strategic word that pulls your heart from its pit of despair or fear and guides your heart to its safe place—the Big "T" Truth. Nevertheless statements tell our hearts, *What you experienced is real; nevertheless, God has something better for you than that!* God's truth gets the ultimate power to define our hearts.

Remember, in order to have true well-being, you can't singularly focus on just your experience, nor just on God's truth.

As you learned in week three, if we just let ourselves get consumed with our experiential reality and forget God's perspective, we're headed for hopelessness and helplessness. On the other hand, if we get consumed with God's perspective and ignore our experiential reality, then we're headed for denial. The Nevertheless Principle helps us avoid both denial

We can rely on one simple word to help our hearts trade our little "t" truths for Big "T" Truth: nevertheless.

and hopelessness/helplessness by creating a dual reality, and carefully reminds our hearts where to put the exclamation point!

The Nevertheless Principle isn't a game of trading realism for blind optimism. This is about inviting God into every experience that needs redefined meaning. This is what unhindered faith should do.

Our minds are renewed when we can see through God's perspective, not our own.

Our minds are renewed when we can see through God's perspective, not our own. It turns rejection into pursuit, defeat into victory, hopelessness into hope, and fear into trust.

When you can't understand, control, or fix it, teach your heart to say, "*Nevertheless*" so God's Word can become the indispensable weapon it's meant to be.

Let this tool make Romans 12:2 your reality, "Do not conform to the pattern of this world, but be transformed by the renewing of your mind. Then you will be able to test and approve what God's will is—his good, pleasing, and perfect will."

Prayer:

God, your voice is more powerful than any other. God, your reality is more true than the reality of this life. God, your Big "T" Truth is the only truth that I want to define my heart.

In my moments of weakness and confusion, help me surrender the untrustworthy messages and remember that, no matter what I feel, there is something more real and true—your voice.

God, your Word truly is an indispensable weapon. Thank you that it always prevails. Amen.

Reflection Questions:

Have you ever found yourself hopeless and helpless—only able to see your circumstances? Or have you ever found yourself in denial—only able to see perspectives of faith? How did that fall short for you?

Write a Nevertheless Statement that brings a difficult experience of yours into relationship with the Truth that prevails over it. What does it feel like to read that out loud? (See Appendix G for examples)

What stood out to you most in today's reading?

The Nevertheless Principle doesn't change our battle, but it is a tool that changes us in the midst of our battle.

DAY 4:

Protecting the New

Momentum has a one-week shelf life.
—ALAN AHLGRIM[19]

I'll never forget the Sunday afternoon when my friend and Children's Pastor at my church, Amanda, (lovingly and humorously!) used me as her human puppet in a demonstration of the importance of Deuteronomy 6:6-9 to a group of parents.

These commandments that I give you today are to be on your hearts. Impress them on your children. Talk about them when you sit at home and when you walk along the road, when you lie down and when you get up. Tie them as symbols on your hands and bind them on your foreheads. Write them on the doorframes of your houses and on your gates.

As an illustration to remind us all to talk with our children about God's Word wherever we go, she asked me to play a toddler

---

19 Alan Ahlgrim, personal conversation with the author.

sitting in her car seat while she played the mother in the front seat of the car. As we "drove" down the imaginary road, she was talking about how much Jesus loves us.

What was Amanda's point? *We must remember.* As parents, we must remember to open our mouths and share Jesus with our kids. We must help our children remember

An old dog really can learn new tricks. Sometimes it just needs a lot of practice.

God's love and Word. We must rehearse and repeat the things God desperately wants us to remember and teach our children so that these truths make their way in their hearts, not just their heads.

It was a little awkward to scrunch my full-grown self into the seat built for a two-year-old that day, but the moment stuck and taught me to remember!

We must help ourselves remember what it takes to live an unhindered life too. Most of us need repeated exposures to the things God is revealing to us for them to begin to redefine us. Our hearts need a lot of prodding to let go of the old things they've been convinced of for so long. An old dog really can learn new tricks. Sometimes it just needs a lot of practice.

After the Israelites defeated the Amalekites in Exodus 17, God instructed Moses who led the victory, "'Write this down on a scroll as a permanent reminder, and read it aloud to Joshua: I will erase the memory of Amalek from under heaven'" (Exodus 17:14).

We cannot let our memories grow faint of the things God can do in our lives when we listen to His voice. So, just like Moses, you need to write down what God is doing in your heart and let your rehearsal of it be a part of the protective plan that guards your heart.

I invite you to create a Remembrance Statement that calls your heart to its new normal (Big "T" Truths and Big "S" Strategies). Ask God, "What do you want me to remember about what is true and how you've called me to live?" This is a very personal question. It's not about opening your Bible to a random page and seeing what general lesson there is to find. This is about God guiding you into the targeted alternative to your unique little "t" truths and small "s" strategies (your old normal) that have made so much sense to you because of the influences and experiences in your life.

Listen to God's inaudible but unmistakable voice in the Bible and in your heart. Sometimes it takes the absence of noise and internal chaos in times of silence and solitude to experience God's presence. Then, you can hear the whispers of His personal invitation to see exactly who you are through His eyes instead of your own. As God reminds you of the new normal He's calling you into, made up of Big "T" Truths and Big "S" Strategies, jot them down. Back them up with Scripture to remind you they aren't just good ideas, they're God's ideas. Then, take all of your notes and put them together in a Remembrance Statement that calls you into a new normal.

We cannot let our memories grow faint of the things God can do in our lives when we listen to His voice.

You can write a Remembrance Statement in two ways:

1) *As a letter written to you by God.*

Write what God is calling you to remember and how He is calling you to live from God's perspective and let it become a personal letter from Him to you. If you choose, use your nickname in the salutation and sign God's name at the bottom to remind you of God's love and presence. You might sign it Abba.

Our hearts need us to consistently feed them truth and lead them with repetition.

You can't assert your own voice as His. But you can use what He says in Scripture to show you what His voice sounds like. You can begin sentences with "I say" or "I long for you to." Include Scripture references as well to remind you of the sovereignty of the words. You'll have the opportunity for His Word to become a personal invitation and promise that comes with the direct authority of His voice. You can be compelled by the urgency and longing God has to see you operating as just who He made you to be.

2) *As a personal declaration.*

You might choose to write a prayer of confession that declares who God says you are and how He is calling you to live. Prayerfully, write this declaration to God as a celebration of, and commitment to, this new way of living.

You can begin sentences that capture your personal Big "T" Truths as "I am" or "I believe" to cover your prayerful statements with authority and power. You can begin sentences that capture Big "S" Strategies inviting you in as "I will" or "I commit to." Include Scripture references in this approach as well to remind you of the authority of the words.

You'll have an opportunity in this method to commit yourself to intentionally walk in the new normal and remind yourself of your personal conviction to do so every time you read it.

Our hearts need us to consistently feed them truth. However, remember that repetition will do you no good until your heart has let the truths become personal (not just head knowledge, but heart knowledge). I encourage you to use this Remembrance Statement as a tool that you read daily, preferably as you begin your

Unhindering your heart is like heart surgery — a spiritual process of inside-out change.

day, to set your heart in your new direction. Let this strategic moment revive your conviction to let go of the old normal and fix your eyes upon the freedom and gifts waiting for you as you consistently align your heart with God.

In addition to intentionally remembering and rehearsing what God has invited you into, be ready to adjust your life for your new normal to fit. You'll need to make sure the rest of your life supports the changes your heart is trying to make. This isn't just about making room for your new normal. It's about propelling your new normal.

Most of us will need healthier rhythms, new disciplines, and a good friend, counselor, or coach to hold us to the commitments we're making to create a new normal.

> *Your gains are real, yet they need your protection.*

Some of us will need to build a life that strategically protects us from sin and internal brokenness. For example, the former alcoholic shouldn't eat their steak at the bar. The former workaholic shouldn't keep working for a boss that requires eighty hours a week, with no excuses allowed. The former body dysmorphic shouldn't fill their social media feed with airbrushed pictures of half-starved models. The former out-of-control spender should not engage in daily shopping trips to Target or Amazon. The formerly walked-on or manipulated person should not reengage in a relationship without clear boundaries put in place.

Why would you keep doing the same things that trigger you left and right and tempt you to the point that you continually open the door to contemplation? Or leave you vulnerable again? You don't need to prove you can handle it. You need to be smart enough to build your life in a way that protects your gains, especially in the beginning.

Unhindering your heart is like heart surgery—a spiritual process of inside-out change. Your heart goes through surgery to heal its "disease" as Sore Spots, Heart Logic, and Private Conclusions are exposed, challenged, and healed. As a postoperative patient, when you finally go home after your hospital stay, you leave with an aftercare plan to keep your physical heart healthy. If you stop eating heart-healthy foods, exercising, and taking the medicine your doctor prescribed, you might be back in the hospital before too long. Likewise, the gains in your heart need to be cared for and continually protected. The real test begins when you get beyond the excitement of a moment of discovery and life settles back into the mundane. Your gains are real, yet they need your protection.

Prayer:

God, I hold the work you are doing in me in such high regard that I will protect it every day. May I never forget the things you are showing my heart to be true. Mark them on my heart and burn them into my memory. God, please fill my daily thoughts with your truth and ways. Thank you for the beauty and freedom you are instilling in me. Amen.

Reflection Questions:

What routine can you get into to rehearse and remember what God is leading you into?

Which version of a Remembrance Statement will fit you best (a letter from God or a personal declaration)? Take some time this week to write it. (See Appendix H for examples)

What stood out to you most in today's reading?

Remember and rehearse.
Adjust and propel.
Protect the beauty of what
God is doing in you.

When Not to Give Up

Sometime later, Jesus went up to Jerusalem for one of the Jewish festivals. Now there is in Jerusalem near the Sheep Gate a pool, which in Aramaic is called Bethesda and which is surrounded by five covered colonnades. Here a great number of disabled people used to lie—the blind, the lame, and the paralyzed. One who was there had been an invalid for thirty-eight years. When Jesus saw him lying there and learned that he had been in this condition for a long time, he asked him, "Do you want to get well?"
—JOHN 5:1-6

In the above passage from John 5, Jesus asked the invalid at the pool this strategic question: "Do you want to get well?" That is a question and invitation for you too.

If you really want to get well, you know a couple of things you have to do by now. You have to fight the series of battles before you. You also have to be patient on the journey of process healing and do your part.

Here are three more pieces of advice to guide you through ongoing healing and growth:

1) *Don't let up too quickly, just when the enemy seems to have retreated.*

One of the biggest mistakes you can make on your journey to an unhindered life is giving up when it starts feeling easy. Just when you think you've got this: you instantly let up your intentional investment in your heart, you get lax on your protective strategies, and you start trusting fragile gains to make it on their own.

> When it starts feeling easy, stay in the new routines and practices that have helped you get well. They'll help you stay well too!

If you relax too soon, your old normal will be right around the corner and will take the invitation to come back in through your unprotected heart. What's the lesson? When it starts feeling easy, stay in the new routines and practices that have helped you get well. They'll help you stay well too!

In many cases you can relax a little over time and let up on the intensity of some of your routines (like rehearsing your Remembrance Statement once a week instead of every day or fewer hours of therapy a month). But be careful not to be fooled by a good week that makes you think you can relent. Remember, this will be a series of battles that must be fought. So, stay ready for the next challenge you'll have to overcome.

2) *Don't give up when you have a setback.*

A setback easily gets misinterpreted as an invalidation of all healing and growth. We think, *I guess it wasn't real or I guess I'm just not capable.* That's not true. Setbacks are simply opportunities for more learning and healing. If you start redefining setbacks as collisions and see them as opportunities, not detractions, your attitude toward them will dramatically change. With that perspective, you can ask yourself, *What can I learn from this? What caught me off guard? What's the next layer of healing you're inviting me into, God?*

After a perceived setback, come back right where you left off. Don't be mistaken by thinking that you have to start back at square one. Listen to the good news from Henry Nouwen:[20]

> *Sometimes little things build up and make you lose ground for a moment. Fatigue, a seemingly cold remark, someone's inability to hear you, someone's innocent forgetfulness, which feels like rejection—when all these come together, they can make you feel as if you are right back where you started. But try to think about it*

Setbacks are simply opportunities for more learning and healing.

20 Henry Nouwen, *The Inner Voice of Love* (New York: Doubleday, 1998), 38.

instead as being pulled off the road for a while. When you return to the road, you return to the place where you left it, not to where you started . . . In everything, keep trusting that God is with you, that God has given you companions on the journey. Keep returning to the road to freedom.

You learned earlier this week that collisions will happen again and again. Working hard to unhinder your heart doesn't mean your intuitive heart won't ever compete again.

Expect that you still might get disappointed or angry with God once in a while. Yet trust that you'll be able to discipline your heart back to seeing His care for you, even in your disappointing circumstances, because of the way He's already lovingly convinced you of who He is through your healing journey.

As you try to embrace your new normal, your mind may try to convince you that it just can't be as good as what you've always known.

Expect that you might still get hurt by people and have your trust broken again. But when you choose to run to the roar, you'll find your way back to seeing these people as broken humans desperately in need of the Savior's grace.

Don't set yourself up for shame and self-condemnation with the wrong expectations that setbacks make you a complete failure. Be gracious with yourself as you unlearn what's been embedded in your heart for decades and relearn something new.

What God has done in you is real, and it can be trusted.

You are now walking on the road to freedom as Nouwen described it. Unexpected setbacks, interruptions on your healing journey, and repeated collisions may take you off course for a moment, but never forget that what you have gained to this point belongs to you and you just get to go take it back.

3) *Don't stop when you get uncomfortable.*

The old normal for your heart has felt as comfortable and attractive as your favorite book. You know it by heart, and you can recite the arc of the story without even seeing the words on the page.

But the new normal for your heart feels like a new book you've never read. The binding feels stiff, and you don't know how it's going to end. You don't even know if you're going to like it.

As you try to embrace your new normal, your mind may try to convince you that it just can't be as good as what you've always known. You might even be tempted to pick up the old normal again and go back to the comfort of your past. But don't listen! You can trust God to write a better story. Courage calls us to choose discomfort because it's the only way to experience the joy and peace of the new, unhindered life God is inviting us into.

Always remember to be gentle with your heart as you challenge it. Unlearning what's been ingrained in you for decades is no small matter. Your heart may still be responding from trauma instincts instead of logic. By the way, that's not an excuse that you can use to get you out of responsibility for hurting someone again with your old ways! But don't judge your heart for its old instincts; be ready to give yourself free-flowing grace.

Don't let up when it starts feeling easy. Don't give up when you have a perceived setback. Don't stop when it feels too uncomfortable. What God has done in you is real and it can be trusted. Reset your heart and keep going! God will strengthen you along the way, giving you assurance that the battle is worth it. Keep walking on the road to freedom.

Prayer:

God, I want to get well! Please strengthen me with the resolve I need to keep going. Help me have grace for myself and not get sidelined by my perceived failures. Help me remain disciplined in moments I'm tempted to give up. Help me trust in your promises in the midst of the battle.

God, thank you for being with me in the ongoing battle for my heart. It is because of you that I can have strength and patience beyond my own. It is because of you that I can have encouragement along my way as I need it. You are so good to me. Amen.

Reflection Questions:

How would you respond to Jesus' question from John 5:6, "Do you want to get well?" Really think about your commitment to those words.

At what point do you tend to give up on things?

What stood out to you most in today's reading?

Don't let up when it starts feeling easy. Don't give up when you have a perceived setback. Don't stop when it feels too uncomfortable.

WEEK 5: GROUP QUESTIONS

1) When might you expect to encounter collisions between your old normal and your new normal? Share what might trigger your old feelings and memories causing you to lose momentary control? How can you be prepared for the moments of battle, so you are ready to take control of them?

2) What is the roar in your life that you've been avoiding? What can motivate you to run into the roar?

3) Share a Nevertheless Statement you've written that brings a difficult experience of yours into relationship with the truth that prevails over it. (See Appendix G for examples)

4) Share what it was like for you to write out your Remembrance Statement (a letter from God or a personal declaration). (See Appendix H for examples)

5) What was your reaction to Jesus' question from John 5:6, "Do you want to get well?" Share what excites you, makes you nervous, or could potentially keep you from making a life-long commitment to unhinder your heart.

WEEK 6:

Living in
The New Normal

DAY 1:

The Unhindered Life

*At last we have freedom, for Christ has set us free!
We must always cherish this truth and firmly refuse
to go back into the bondage of our past.*
—GALATIANS 5:1 (TPT)

*Therefore, since we are surrounded by such a great cloud of
witnesses, let us throw off everything that hinders and the sin
that so easily entangles. And let us run with perseverance the
race marked out for us, fixing our eyes on Jesus, the pioneer
and perfecter of faith. For the joy set before him he endured
the cross, scorning its shame, and sat down at the right hand of
the throne of God. Consider him who endured such opposition
from sinners, so that you will not grow weary and lose heart.*
—HEBREWS 12:1-3

Slow down and read the scriptures above again.

Use this time to sit with the Holy Spirit. Take a few deep
breaths as you still yourself.

Reflect on the story you have been crafting the past five weeks.

If I was with you in person, I would celebrate the hard work you have done, because heart work is always worth celebrating!

There is *beauty* and *freedom* in aligning your heart with God and "throwing off everything that hinders and the sin that so easily entangles." As you refuse to go back, there is more living unleashed, not held back. More living free and light, not weighed down. More living that is guided by Godly wisdom, not fear and protection. I hope you are already feeling some of this freedom on your unhindered journey, but just know there is even more that awaits.

Living unhindered brings us a step closer to the image of Jesus. We love more deeply. We trust more readily. We lean on God's wisdom more than our own understanding. We don't run from conflict, but instead, we engage with a beautiful blend of grace and truth. We let go of our agenda and expectations and accept the invitation to join God on His amazing, yet unpredictable journey.

Living unhindered brings us a step closer to the image of Jesus.

The unhindered life is a life of beautiful dependence on God, which means a life of rest for us.

Psalm 91:1-2 says it like this, "Whoever dwells in the shelter of the Most High will rest in the shadow of the Almighty. I will say of the Lord, He is my refuge and my fortress, my God, in whom I trust."

An incredible work of art is emerging as we enter living unhindered. As we allow God to take over the canvas of our lives, we will enter our *full poten-tial—our emerging genius.* Remember from week two, our true genius isn't our intelligence, our ability to succeed, or our capacity to innovate. Our genius is living to the fullest capacity of our spiritual DNA.

Though this DNA is unique in its expression in each one of us, each of our emerging geniuses is similar in that it is marked by a *strength* that will help us "run with perseverance the race marked out for us." It might take a little time before you feel strength arise, but it's coming!

The unhindered life is a life of beautiful dependency on God which means a life of rest for us.

At first, the unhindered life might feel foreign, like a book you're reading in Arabic (assuming you don't speak Arabic). But over time your instincts will shift, and your thoughts will change. This new life will become your new normal. As you start to trust the new normal of your unhindered heart, you'll find your confidence grow and notice you have the strength to carry out this new way of living. You will step into places you would have once thought were too scary. You will do things you wouldn't have thought you were qualified for. You will live less afraid and less intimidated.

You will be more alive and free than ever!

Without unhindering my heart, the last few years of my life would not have happened as they have. My dad turned the leadership of Blessing Ranch Ministries over to me in 2017. It was a move I didn't see coming and would have never asked for. I'll never forget the moment after the proposal was made, in a Board of

Directors meeting, that we stop looking for new leadership outside of the organization and put me in that seat. I sat there quietly while seven sets of expectant eyes turned my direction and bore down on me.

My immediate instinct was to freeze, panic inside, and say, *Not me! I'm not equipped. I'm not enough. I can't do that.* But then, I had a second thought. Somewhere in the back of my mind arose the trustworthy voice of the Holy Spirit that challenged me and said, *Charity, is this intimidating, or are you just intimidated?*

As we allow God to take over the canvas of our lives, we will enter our full potential —— our emerging genius.

My little "t" truth had been caught, and the voice of insecurity was called out! Because I no longer trust that voice of insecurity in me to determine my steps, I chose to say, *Yes, God, I'll step into this unfamiliar and intimidating place of leadership. I have so much to learn, but I know You will help me and equip me.*

As Will unhindered his heart, he also found himself in new, unfamiliar territory.

Will grew up in a small town and church where everyone wore a happy face, pretended that no one was hindered, and brushed any hurt and pain under the rug. That meant that he'd minimized the physical abuse and threats he, along with the rest of his family, had faced from his dad almost daily growing up. Years later, after feeling prompted by God, he found the courage to disrupt that old normal of covering up by getting honest with his family about what happened as a child. Will wanted his mom and sister to know that the mistreatment was real and that it had made lasting impact on his heart. He knew that it had on their hearts too, and he couldn't stand to see them left so hindered.

There was a lot at stake if he didn't speak up. Will was increasingly finding himself angry, just like his dad. He had to do something different and get honest about what was pent up inside of him. He had to take control of the anger before it hurt others around him like he'd been hurt by his dad's unmanaged anger.

What was also at stake if he didn't speak up was everyone's chance to become unhindered. This wasn't about getting back at his dad or purposelessly causing trouble in the family. It was about facing the painful reality of the past, so there could be healing, a chance to say "no" to the old and unhealthy strategy of cover-up, and an opportunity to try to bring his family into more vulnerable and real relationships.

I wish I could say that he received empathy, validation, and encouragement from everyone for doing the work to unhinder his heart and get honest with them about the truth. Unfortunately, his mom wasn't ready to face the truth and kept up her routine of making excuses for her husband's anger. She wouldn't listen. But Will's sister did. What a gift it was to her to have someone finally put words to the things she'd never allowed herself to fully acknowledge. It was the catalyst to her journey to unhinder herself.

Charity, is this intimidating or are you just intimidated?

Although Will knew that speaking out might bring some lasting challenges, he chose to stand upon his new-found security that was not dependent on other people's validation. Trusting his new normal, Will was able to find the confidence to speak even when it might not be received and say, "I trust you, God, with what you ask me to do."

No matter the outcome of his circumstance, his coura- geous obedience was an act of faith, a demonstration of strength, and a declaration of his new-found freedom to face reality. Even though it all didn't turn out ideally with everyone in the family on board with authenticity, it was worth it. It was worth it for Will because he was obedient to his new Big "S" Strategy of living vulnerably before others, and he took control of the roots of his anger. It was also worth it to give that gift of freedom to his sister and to plant a seed for his mom. Just maybe that seed will grow one day.

There's even more beauty in an unhindered life than you can imagine.

Ephesians 3:20 (NLT) says, "Now all glory to God, who is able, through his mighty power at work within us, to accom- plish infinitely more than we might ask or think." When we are strengthened by security in God's love and presence, ruthless trust, and unshakable hope, we become capable of doing things and enduring things we would have never dreamed.

There's even more beauty in an *unhindered* life than you can imagine. It is as close as we'll get to knowing the joy of heavenly life, while still existing in the bounty of brokenness and disappoint- ments of this world. These words are true: "In this world you will have trouble. But take heart! I have overcome the world" (John 16:33b, NIV).

Life is difficult. Period. If we try to ignore pain in an effort to make life easy, we will always fail and be disappointed and defeated. The goal is to purposefully live well and lead our hearts well in a world that is difficult and temporary, so that we finish our race well. The good news is that God has given us unlimited access to what our hearts need for this to be said of our lives. That is something to celebrate!

Prayer:

God, thank you for the chance to live an unhindered life! You always have a way to lead me beyond where I've been and what I've known. Thank you for the promise that we can do more than we could ever ask or imagine when we're in it with you.

Let my character, love for others, and intimacy with you be the evidence of the work you've done in my life. May I say "yes" to you even more often when I'm out of my own way. Make me a blessing to others because of what you've done in me. Amen.

Reflection Questions:

What are you looking forward to the most in your unhindered life?

What challenge might you say "yes" to if you had more confidence or strength? Could God be in that situation?

What stood out to you most in today's reading?

Living with an unhindered heart brings out the best in us so we can rise to the occasion before us.

DAY 2:

Emotional and Spiritual Health

Defensiveness and self-reliance keep us from the adventure of joining with Jesus to change the world.
—JOHN WALKER, PH.D., BLESSING RANCH MINISTRIES

Today, let's celebrate the access we gain to emotional and spiritual health when we unhinder our hearts! As you saw in week three, an unhindered heart creates unhindered faith, and unhindered faith makes us emotionally and spiritually strong. We find strength to overcome a challenge, endure ongoing suffering, and love as Jesus loves. That's the essence of wellness and health!

Without emotional and spiritual health, we're in trouble.

Blow-ups rarely have to do with intellectual deficits. The implosion of a leadership team rarely has to do with a skill deficit. A moral failure isn't likely due to only an accountability deficit.

These things have everything to do with emotional and spiritual deficits. These deficits, buried in our hearts, oppose our emotional and spiritual maturity and get in the way of our health. Skills and strategies won't fix it. Only God's liberating work within our hearts can heal what is broken.

You can't be spiritually well without being emotionally well.

Here's the reality: "Emotional health and spiritual maturity are inseparable. It is not possible to be spiritually mature while remaining emotionally immature."[21]

You can't be spiritually well without being emotionally well.

How can you live surrendered to Jesus when you have a trust problem? *You can't.*

How can you love your neighbor as yourself when your pride keeps you too self-focused? *You won't.*

How are you an example of Jesus when you are too afraid of people's opinions to let them see your faith on display? *You aren't.*

Too often, we expect that learning the Bible, increasing spiritual knowledge, and doing things for God will make us into disciples that mirror Jesus. Then we wonder why we are still stuck in our old sin patterns or with our hang-ups after having a salvation experience, attending church events, and even joining a serving team.

---

21 Peter Scazzero, *Emotionally Healthy Spirituality* (Nashville: Thomas Nelson, 2006).

We have to deal with the misaligned parts of our hearts that are inadvertently resisting who Jesus wants us to become. It might be the Sore Spot of pride that keeps us on the "throne" instead of letting God rightfully be there. It might be the shame that keeps us in a self-punishing cycle instead of walking in grace. Just like lungs need air, spiritual health must be catalyzed by an emotionally healthy heart.

Keep in mind that the pathway to wellness can't ignore the need for spiritual health either.

How can you have lasting hope when you've faced a tragic loss if you don't have the assurance of God creating purpose from the pain? Temporal hope will fail you when you need hope the most.

How can you be secure in who you are if all you have to define that security is winning the comparison game? Someone will eventually beat you.

How can you fully separate yourself from the anger that's controlled you until the grace and mercy of Jesus flow through your veins? You'll have to exist on gentleness found through willpower, not the natural outpouring of faith within you.

> We have to deal with the misaligned parts of our hearts that are inadvertently resisting who Jesus wants us to become.

As you pursue the development of both emotional and spiritual health, you must remember that health doesn't come from just receiving information and inspiration. It comes from supernatural transformation. Your healing will always fall one step short if Jesus hasn't been a part of it.

> *Your healing will always fall one step short if Jesus hasn't been a part of it.*

That's why the pathway toward more freedom, strength, and health cannot just be to pray and read your Bible more. That *is* a good approach. Actually, it's essential. But until you attend to your hindered heart and partner with God to get the opposition out of the way, your health, your strength, and your life will be hindered too.

Growth and healing take place because God's truth and love have provided an alternative to the pain or faulty lessons that life taught. As you learn to open up your emotional world and reveal the pain, misguided learnings, and fears that exist within you, God's truth and love must be the medicine that gets applied. A superficial, one-time application will not be enough. It must run deep. It must make its way into your identity, into the core beliefs that define you, and into the deepest parts of your pain. This is how you will be changed from the inside out.

I hope you are coming to terms with the fact that *emotional and spiritual health cannot be separated*. When we simultaneously pursue them in a transformative way, we've found the keys to *real* health. Their coexistence gives strength and perseverance to our character, joy, and unconditional love.

Not only does the collision between emotional and spiritual maturation produce true health, it also produces true self. Your emotionally and spiritually healthy self is your most authentic self. As you lay down your hindrances, the Holy Spirit will begin to define you more than your flesh. Eventually, your instincts will become more consistent with what's good, noble, and Godly. This is when you become your most authentic self, the person God always intended you to be.

Emotional and spiritual health are not just luxuries to chase when you have time. They are not just extra credit for those who want to be the best in the class. They are the essence of a Christian life that allow us to emulate Jesus wherever we go.

Let's celebrate the pathway to emotional and spiritual health that creates lasting wellness and brings out our authentic selves!

God's truth and love must be the medicine that gets applied. A superficial, one-time application will not be enough. It must run deep.

Prayer:

God, thank you for showing me how much you care about every part of me. I don't have to deny my heart to be strong in you. I get to open my heart to you and let you fill me with your love, comfort, and assurances to make me well. Let my faith come alive even more as my heart is unhindered. God, let me be an example of both emotional and spiritual health to those around me and inspire others to chase after the fullness of life they can find through their relationship with you. Amen.

Reflection Questions:

Have you paid more attention to your emotional or spiritual health? What would it look like to pursue them simultaneously?

Can you identify ways that your limited emotional health has negatively impacted your spiritual health? How would greater emotional health change your spiritual health?

How would you describe the differences between having information, inspiration, and transformation?

What stood out to you most in today's reading?

Emotional and spiritual health are non-negotiables to the unhindered life of a believer.

The Equipment

Unhealed wounds require our attention, and we will have trouble focusing on others while those wounds still need attention. This causes many of us to miss our destinations, on a routine basis, that over a lifetime produce our destiny.[22]
—JOHN LYNCH, BRUCE MCNICHOL, AND BILL THRALL

Today, let's celebrate the blessing you become when you are unhindered! God certainly wants you to enjoy the freedom and ease of an unhindered life (John 10:10). But it's not all about you!

As Jesus sent out His twelve disciples to care for others and heal in His name in Matthew 10, He said to them, "Don't think you have to put on a fund-raising campaign before you start. You don't need a lot of equipment. You are the equipment, and all you need to keep that going is three meals a day. Travel light" (Matthew 10:9-10, MSG).

---

22 John Lynch, Bruce McNichol, and Bill Thrall, *The Cure: What If God Isn't Who You Think He Is and Neither are You?* (Phoenix: Trueface, 2011).

Jesus refers to His disciples as "equipment." They were the hands and feet of the gospel, sent out as change agents to sow, plant, cultivate, and harvest. With their trust and hope in Jesus and nothing else, they would bring about change.

As we live unhindered and travel light with our trust and hope solely in Jesus, we too become the equipment He will use to incite change in the world around us.

1) *We become change-makers in our families.*

Psalm 145:4-5 (TPT) says, "Generation after generation will declare more of your greatness and declare more of your glory. Your magnificent splendor and the miracles of your majesty are my constant meditation."

As we live unhindered, we sow more love and security into our family which is our greatest responsibility. Our spouses (or future spouses) can feel more loved as patience and gentleness become our instincts. Our kids (or those who see us as parental figures) can feel more affirmed and secure as we embrace the chaos and noise that childhood energy brings, remain calm in the uncertainty of raising teenagers, and let go of unnecessary expectations that

As we live unhindered and travel light with our trust and hope solely in Jesus, we too become the equipment He will use to incite change in the world around us.

we have of our grown children.

We can change the trajectory for future generations in our families too. The choice we make to leave behind a pattern of criticism may protect our grandchildren from ever knowing the plague of the internal voice that says, "You're never enough." The internal work we do can break the pattern of surface-level-only connections in our families and can lead to greater emotional and spiritual connection and maturity in the generations to come.

As we live unhindered, we sow more love and security into our family which is our greatest responsibility.

2) *We become change-makers in our churches.*

1 Corinthians 12:18-20 (TPT) says, "But God has carefully designed each member and placed it in the body to function as he desires. A diversity is required, for if the body consisted of one single part, there wouldn't be a body at all! So now we see that there are many differing parts and functions, but one body."

John 17:22-23 says, "I have given them the glory that you gave me, that they may be one as we are one—I in them and you in me—so that they may be brought to complete unity. Then the world will know that you sent me and have loved them even as you have loved me."

We all have a unique part to play in the body of Christ. While we can evoke change by using our gifts, talents, and resources to grow the church, John tells us that God desires unity and that our unity will ultimately show the world the love of our Heavenly Father. While we cannot demand unity in our

Without a healthy you, the body doesn't operate to the fullest of its potential.

churches, we can unify ourselves with God's truth, live unhindered, and trust God to do what only He can do in the lives and hearts of others.

Your part in this matters in the life of your church. Maybe you are the person your church-averse neighbor trusts enough to listen to. Maybe you are the only one who will connect with the teenager who everyone else runs from! Maybe you are the only one who has just the right background to help shape the vision for community impact.

Without a healthy you, the body doesn't operate to the fullest of its potential.

3) *We become change-makers in our world.*

Matthew 28:18-20 (TPT) says, "All authority of the universe has been given to me. Now wherever you go, make disciples of all nations, baptizing them in the name of the Father, the Son, and the Holy Spirit. And teach them to faithfully follow all that I have commanded you. And never forget that I am with you every day, even to the completion of this age."

The command of Jesus to go and make disciples of all nations tells us that the goal for each of us is to become a disciple of Christ. So, what exactly is a disciple? By simple definition, a disciple is a student or follower of Jesus. But there's a big difference between a disciple and a *healthy* disciple.

Sure, we can be disciples of Jesus with hindrances in our hearts, neglecting our emotional and spiritual health. However, we should resolve to become *healthy* disciples who have had our hindrances unlocked to put on display the freedom and strength that come from making Jesus the true Lord of our lives.

As we become unhindered from our trials, struggles, heartaches, and/or hang-ups, our experience can become a rich blessing to our families, churches, and the world. Our story of God's faithfulness can be passed down for generations, gifted to others in our community, and to a world who needs Jesus.

The impact we make on the lives of others will mirror the impact God has made in our lives. As we unhinder our hearts, we gain access to the best job ever—to bless those around us with our greater character, love, mercy, and leadership.

Let your genius (the best of you) come alive so you can show up and be the change agent you were meant to be.

Prayer:

God, you say that I am your equipment. Thank you for letting me be a part of your amazing purposes! Show me how you want to use me. I want to be available to you to serve, love, and bless others and make the unique contribution you want me to make. Prompt my heart and stir my spirit when you need me to act, speak up, start a conversation, or share a smile. Show me your desires for how I invest my time and energy. I want to be used by you in powerful ways to be your agent for change. Amen.

Reflection Questions:

What kind of difference maker are you called to be?

How do you hope that living an unhindered life will help or change others around you?

What stood out to you most in today's reading?

As I unhinder my heart, God will turn my pain into purpose and use me as His "equipment" to evoke change in my family, my church, and the world at large.

DAY 4:

Aligning with God

*Trust in the Lord completely, and do not rely on your own
opinions. With all your heart rely on him to guide you, and he
will lead you in every decision you make. Become intimate with
him in whatever you do, and he will lead you wherever you go.*
—PROVERBS 3:5-6 (TPT)

Now that we've celebrated and fully appreciated the beauty
of God's invitation to an unhindered life, let's remember
the pathway He's given us to do it: unhinder our hearts to
unhinder our lives.

It's time to pull together all we've learned about what that process
looks like and what it takes.

Over the last several weeks, we've been coming face to face with
the intricate pieces of ourselves:

- Heart Shapers

- Sore Spots

- Heart Logic (Is God good? Are you? Others? Life?)

- Private Conclusions (little "t" truths/Big "T" Truths and small "s" strategies/Big "S" Strategies)

- Life Outcomes

These pieces come together to create our heart's story, our story.

Did you know that there's a story within you? Just like a good novel, the drama, challenge, or problem that happens early in our stories creates the tension that exists in the following chapters. Each

The story of our hearts writes the story of our lives.

piece of our heart builds on the last, just as chapters of a book build a story arc. And just like in most stories, it takes a hero (in our case, God) to change the trajectory from inevitable doom (or even second best) to beauty and strength.

As you know by now, you can't fully understand the ending of your story until you understand the beginning. The story of our hearts writes the story of our lives. There is no separating the two.

In this final week of learning the pathway to unhinder ourselves from all that holds us back, it's important that we pull together all of the essential pieces and begin to see them as a cohesive story. We will take a little bit of time this week to remember what we've learned, connect the dots, and write the story of our own hearts.

Let's look at Eli's story to help us see how all of the pieces of his hindered heart told a story that needed to be rewritten by God.

Baseball was the best and worst Heart Shaper in Eli's life. All the drills he didn't want to do and the responsibility to not let the team down taught him to do the right thing and keep working hard even when he didn't feel like it anymore. He wouldn't trade that! But baseball shaped his heart in a not-so-helpful way too. It taught him that everything is a competition, and he had better win. He wanted to win so badly—whether winning the game or having the best stats of the day—because it's what got him attention.

It felt so good to him to be noticed, especially as a kid from a family of four who was always vying to be noticed at home (another Heart Shaper). He was absolutely loved at home, but something in him wanted more. That may have been, in part, because of another Heart Shaper. The church he grew up in was pretty legalistic and full of "rules" to follow that made you "good enough." *"Make sure you are at church on Sunday morning, Sunday night, and Wednesday night. If you aren't, you're disappointing God."* *"You have to always act properly to be a good Christian, and that means no music other than Christian music, stay away from girls, and always have the right clothes on."*

Just when he thought he was getting one expectation under control, they would throw on another shaming message that put him right back in that spot of fearing God and judgment, so Eli resolved to know that he was going to fail the expectations of the church. Baseball became his "everything" because he knew he could win there. He had enough grit and talent to sometimes hit the home run that brought him the cheers his heart longed to hear.

Through all these Heart Shapers, Sore Spots of insecurity and shame found a home, telling Eli that he wasn't enough. A Sore

Spot of fear was there too, telling him to fear losing approval and people's regard.

Some of Eli's Heart Logic was undoubtedly affected. He couldn't say, *"Yes, God is good all the time"* because the fear he had of God's judgment didn't make him feel very safe. It made him feel more like God was just a moment away from furrowing His brow and shaking His head in dis-

Don't ever underestimate the power of a little misalignment.

appointment. God was a greedy boss, not a good Father. Eli couldn't say, *"Yes, I am good even though I'm flawed"* because he was dependent on the praise and attention he got from baseball to feel good enough. That feeling of security he got after a great game didn't last long before the need to earn the next round of applause returned.

Eli went through life with Private Conclusions shaped by his mis-aligned heart. Little "t" truths ruled him. *Maybe if you become a ministry leader, you'll finally prove to all these people at church and to God that you are good enough to belong. As long as I keep improving and outperforming what I did last year, I'll be okay.*

So, Eli's small "s" strategy of choice was to *achieve*. Long after baseball faded from his life, he went into ministry to try to prove something and he made his performance there his new idol. He was always the one on staff who wasn't satisfied with things being excellent—they had to be better than they were before. He was always second-guessing where he stood with his boss, and he was prone to make up stories about his boss's disappointment that didn't match reality. Because of that, the other small "s" strategy he fell vulnerable to was people pleasing. Eli would spend so much wasted energy trying to make up for whatever he had "failed" at, when he hadn't actually failed anyone.

This got the best of him over time as he grew more anxious about meeting expectations as the stakes got higher in his job. It was hard for him to relax and wind down, even when he had a day off. His anxiety was a negative Life Outcome that was robbing him.

Another tough impact this all had on Eli was being vulnerable to the attention of another female staff member. Eli wasn't married, but she was, and Eli knew it. Yet her attention and affirmations felt so good to him, so he kept letting her in closer. He didn't mean to! He would not have ever wanted to disrupt a family like that. But before he realized what was happening, they were exchanging texts that she was hiding from her husband. Then they were meeting up after work alone. Then they were kissing. Then they were caught. Another Life Outcome for Eli was that his character was compromised. He had traded his integrity for affirmation.

Eli's heart had been misaligned with God, and that misaligned his life. Heart Shapers that many people would brush off as "not a big deal," "normal," or "just the way it was" had a lot of power to bring misalignment into his life.

Don't ever underestimate the power of a little misalignment. If your car's tires are out of alignment, at first you might notice just a slight pull to the right as you drive down the highway. You might brush it off, just course correcting with a minor compensation of the wheel. As you leave the tire misalignment unchecked for months though, the misalignment grows. It begins to feel like a magnetic pull tugging your car toward the shoulder of the road. If you aren't paying attention, you'll find yourself in the ditch, wondering how you got there.

A little misalignment can go a long way.

Just like Eli, if you have a misaligned heart, influenced by Sore Spots and faulty Heart Logic, you will be hindered by little "t" truths and small "s" strategies that will guide your life off the course that God has set and sometimes lead you all the way into the ditch.

Thankfully, Eli got curious about his heart and partnered with God to align his heart and realign his life. The pathway Eli chose is the very same one that's been offered to you.

After the exposure of his inappropriate relationship with the married woman, Eli came face to face with the trajectory of his life that he now despised. The first thing Eli had to do was get the recipe right for how to change his life's trajectory. Eli had to accept that he couldn't just apologize and put up a few boundaries with the married woman and expect all to be well again. That would have been putting a Band-Aid on the problem. He had to learn to get to the heart of the matter—his own heart. With some help from a counselor, he began to recognize that there was something within him—his hindrances—that were a big part of compelling him to compromise his character and create the anxiety that was leaving him on edge all the time. He was empowered as he began to realize that he wasn't helpless to the hindrances!

When Eli's heart aligned with God, his life aligned with God.

With the perspective that pointed him toward the kind of inside-out healing that could truly change his trajectory, Eli was ready to peel back the layers of his heart and get to the root.

He faced the Heart Shapers in his life that had left their mark as Sore Spots. The hardest part for him was to admit that his church had been a negative influence on his life because admitting that felt like doing something wrong. He finally accepted that acknowledging the hard side of things didn't risk his standing with God.

Eli worked to unhinder his heart by trading his Sore Spots of insecurity, shame, and fear for the comfort of God's love, acceptance, and assurance. Eli had to let God's voice become louder than all the other unsatisfied voices of his past (including his own) that seemed to always want one more expectation met. That took moments of solitude with God where Eli meditated on God's character and heart toward him. He did a lot of journaling where he affirmed these things to be true for him, not just everyone else. He even reimagined moments of his past where he'd heard the voice of shame or fear and visualized God in those moments speaking Big "T" Truth over and above the perceived message of the lived moment.

As his Sore Spots lost their influence, Eli could get rid of his exceptions to the Heart Logic questions and emphatically said, "yes" to each of God's promises of goodness. Eli could say, "Yes, God is good all the time" now that he could trust that God is not waiting to furrow His brow, but is instead waiting with open arms. He reexamined his answer to the question, "Am I good even though I'm flawed?" with the assurance that, because of Jesus, he measured up. As Eli let God remake his self-image and God-image, he took a deep breath and settled into the security it brought him. Finally, he could accept that he is enough without needing anyone or anything to validate that. He's enough simply because God said it's true and because the Spirit lives in him, covering his faults with the grace of God and his weaknesses with the strength of God (2 Corinthians 12:9-10, Romans 8:38-39).

Through that process of aligning his heart with God by healing Sore Spots and rewriting Heart Logic, his heart could be filled with the ingredients of faith: security, ruthless trust, and unshakable hope. Eli's faith was unhindered, and that began to show up in how he lived.

Eli could now surrender his little "t" thinking and small "s" strategies that unwittingly opposed God. He could adopt the wisdom and peace of Private Conclusions defined by Big "T" thinking and Big "S" Strategies. For Eli, that meant standing on Big "T" Truths like, *I've got nothing to prove! Hitting my goal, getting the promotion, or impressing someone isn't necessary for God to smile on me; only my faithfulness is* (Ephesians 2:8-9, Deuteronomy 7:9). *God can do good and worthy things that can't always be measured by stats, numbers and exceeded goals, so I can trust whatever agenda He might have for my life and work.*

As you liberate yourself from unhealthy alignment with the ascribed values of culture, the untrustworthy lessons from your family of origin, or what you think will please people, you sync up with God's every original intention, thought, and way.

These Big "T" Truths guided him out of his heart's misguided motivations for self-protection and avoidance of pain through achievement and pleasing people (small "s" strategies). Instead, he sought Big "S" Strategies of simply serving (doing whatever God asked without it being for self-gain) and pleasing God alone (honoring others while not elevating his standing with others over his standing with God).

When Eli's heart aligned with God, his life aligned with God. The amplified emotional and spiritual strength within him brought strength out of him! In his new strength, anxieties could relax because there wasn't anything to prove anymore (2 Timothy 1:7, Psalm 94:19). Integrity could become his again as he repented and planted his heart back in the values he's always held—now without the thwarting influence of a fearful and insecure heart (1 John 1:9, Psalm 25:21). *Eli arrived in unhindered living!*

It's the same for you as it was for Eli. As you liberate yourself from unhealthy alignment with the ascribed values of culture, the untrustworthy lessons from your family of origin, or what you think will please people, you sync up with God's every original intention, thought, and way. Your identity matches how He sees you and your view of God mirrors who He says He is. You see others as He does, you run on faith made up of security, trust, and hope, and you do the things that He says will bring you life. You become strong just as Eli became strong! Remember, strength doesn't mean you don't have to battle for your heart anymore because it no longer gets triggered or weary at times. Strength just means you have the capacity to find victory in those battles by finding your way back to the unhindered life God has set your course toward. You grow even more through the battles. That emotional and spiritual strength will save you, too, from being pulled into the ditch. It will keep the road feeling smooth even when you're driving over potholes. *That deserves a celebration!*

I hope that walking through Eli's story has helped cement your understanding of how all the pieces of your heart's story weave together to create a unified storyline. I hope it also helped you see even more clearly that you have to rewrite the whole story from beginning to end to turn it from a tragic story (or just a bore) into a page turner whose ending you can't wait to see.

Keep in mind that Eli's story isn't a story of just returning to the way it used to be. It's a story about finding a new normal, a whole new level of freedom and authenticity. Eli took the next step up in his character and freed himself from the vulnerabilities that could have caught him unguarded again one day. It's a story of rising strength!

Prayer:

God, I want to celebrate all that you are showing me about what it looks like to become more like you. No matter how long I've walked with you, there's always more alignment with you that I long for.

God, you can write a better story than anyone. I trust that as I surrender my old normal and step into the new with you, that I can trust the story you'll write. Amen.

Reflection Questions:

Take some time to reflect on the idea that all the pieces of your heart weave together to tell a story. Can you begin to see how the dots connect?

Please use the "TUL Pathway" diagram (See Appendix J) to write out the pieces of your heart's story. Use it to practice telling the story of your heart and how God wants to rewrite the story.

How can you begin to see the beauty, freedom, and strength that will emerge in your unhindered story?

What stood out to you most in today's reading?

Each piece of your heart's story comes together to write the story of your life.

DAY 5:

The Tools That Unhinder You

*For although we live in the natural realm, we don't wage
a military campaign employing human weapons, using
manipulation to achieve our aims. Instead, our spiritual
weapons are energized with divine power to effectively
dismantle the defenses behind which people hide.*
—2 CORINTHIANS 10:3-4 (TPT)

God has asked us to let Him become our Heart Shaper—to let Him reclaim the influence that imperfect life experiences and pain have unrightfully taken. Yesterday, you saw the powerful exchanges Eli made of the misalignments in his heart and life for alignment with God. "But how exactly did he do it?" That's usually the follow-up question. We need practical ways to give God the opportunities He longs for: to address our pain, to teach our hearts that they can trust His love and truth more than their experience, to reshape our perspectives, and to create a new normal.

As we talked about in week five, God equips us with meaningful weapons for our battles like prayer, His Word, and His help. We just need to know how to use these weapons wisely so they can make the difference in our hearts.

Over the last few weeks, we have learned several tools to engage those Godly weapons in ways that really can transform our hearts and subsequently help them stay firm. Let's pull together the tools we've learned (and add one or two more) that lead us into an unhindered life.

God has asked us to let Him become our Heart Shaper — to let Him reclaim the influence that imperfect life experiences and pain have unrightfully taken.

There are several phases on our journeys of unhindering our lives, and there are specific tools to have in each phase that will be helpful.

Phase One: *Discovery*

In the beginning of your journey to live unhindered, it might have felt strange to pay attention to your heart. Maybe you've felt like a fish out of water, perhaps not knowing where to begin to name your Sore Spots or call out your little "t" truths. For most of you, this was probably the first time you've examined specific pieces of your heart like its Heart Shapers or Heart Logic. Maybe you've longed for some direction and help to see what you can't see. You might want to ask a friend or a counselor to point out your blind spots. Don't forget to ask God to show you what He sees too. That's where a tool called *Searching Prayer* can help.

Searching prayer may also serve you well, even if you think you already know yourself well. Keep in mind that you might still have things to discover. We need to be disarmed from defenses and pride and armed with a whole lot of curiosity and take that posture into *Searching Prayer.*

Searching Prayer:

Psalm 139:1-6 (NLT) says, "O Lord, you have examined my heart and know everything about me. You know when I sit down or stand up. You know my thoughts even when I'm far away. You see me when I travel and when I rest at home. You know everything I do. You know what I am going to say even before I say it, Lord. You go before me and follow me. You place your hand of blessing on my head. Such knowledge is too wonderful for me, too great for me to understand!"

God has already examined our hearts and knows it all. So, if we have questions about what is within us, wouldn't it make sense to ask Him to show us?

Psalm 139:23-24 (NLT) affirms that, "Search me, O God, and know my heart; test me and know my anxious thoughts. Point out anything in me that offends you, and lead me along the path of everlasting life."

Searching Prayer is an opportunity for you to lay down everything you think you know about yourself, everything you have discovered so far on this journey, and ask God to show you what He sees. What pain can He see in your heart that you've been too defensive to notice? What exception does He see you making to a Heart Logic question from which you've excused yourself? What little "t" truth needs to be dismantled? What small "s" strategy have you become so accustomed to that you need God's help to illuminate its danger and source?

Prepare for Searching Prayer by getting into a quiet space, free of distractions. Empty your mind of its chaos by writing down the to-do list that is calling your name or handing something to God to manage for a moment while you shift your attention away from it.

Reflect on the questions below that you have hopefully already begun to answer in previous chapters.

God has already examined our hearts and knows it all. So, if we have questions about what is within us, wouldn't it make sense to ask Him to show us?

You can turn back in your book to the Reflection Questions you've completed or refer to Appendix J to remind you of your answers. Maybe you can even write them from memory now.

Pose each question before God once more. Ask Him again to show you what is within you. Then, take on the most important part: listen! Stay quiet and tune in to what else God might want to show you. Pay attention to what comes into your awareness.

What major life events or influences come to mind that have shaped your heart from your childhood, adolescence, and adult life?

What Sore Spot did a Heart Shaper create in you? What Sore Spot within you needs more unpacking? (fear, shame, rejection, pride, inadequacy/insecurity, feeling unvalued)

What Heart Logic question are you still hesitating to answer, "Yes!"? (God, Me, Others, Life)

What little "t" truths have you believed, maybe even unknowingly?

What small "s" strategies have you lived out of these little "t" truths, maybe even unknowingly?

Phase Two: *Healing*
Healing encompasses thousands of individualized ways we need to recover from the Sore Spots we've been left with. There's not one universal tool to leave you with for healing.

There is certainly one that might serve you on that healing journey: *Entrusting.*

Entrusting:

Entrusting means to turn something over to someone else to care for, protect, or manage well for us. We entrust our money into stocks, expecting return on investment. We entrust our kids to our babysitters, expecting them to be kept safe and be fed. Likewise, we can entrust our hearts to God.

First Peter 2:22-23 (TPT) gives us a model of "entrusting" in a spiritual sense: "He never sinned and he never spoke deceitfully. When he was verbally abused, he did not return with an insult; when he suffered, he would not threaten retaliation. Jesus faithfully entrusted himself into the hands of God, who judges righteously."

We, too, must entrust the unjust to God. Many of us have betrayal stored up in our hearts. Many have a rejection that has felt so unfair. Some of us have been left unprotected by those who were supposed to keep us safe. Some of us just didn't get the love or connection that we would have expected. Entrusting all of that hurt and injustice doesn't mean that

We too, must entrust the unjust to God.

we expect God to right all of our wrongs in the here and now. It does mean that we trust Him to manage them well, by holding it for us so we don't have to, by sometimes bringing earthly justice, or by working healing into our offender's life.

The practice of entrusting can take many forms. One of those can be a simple prayer with a visualization attached. Close your eyes and place your hands before you, palms open. Imagine the person, event, or wound you need to entrust sitting in your hands. Now, picture God before you, arms outstretched ready to receive from you. Watch the exchange happen between you as you pray, "God, I entrust_____ (fill in the blank with your situation) to you. I release the pain, the responsibility, or the injustice to you. I trust you to manage it well."

Entrusting things to God is a piece of freeing our hearts from resentment and responsibility to fix it or understand it. It's an acceptance of God's loving care over a circumstance that has left us in pain. It's an act of trust that reorients our hearts with knowing that we are loved by God when the world didn't show it, that we are safe in God's care when injustice still exists, and that we don't need all the wrongs to be righted in order to soften our hearts toward others again or let go of control.

Phase Three: *Getting Convinced of Truth*
God's love and truth do you no good if they're stuck in your head and blocked from your heart. You have learned that you have to

fight for these things to become your experience, so you actually live them and not just know them.

To get convinced, you have to guide your heart to let go of over relying on intuitive experiences and feelings and receive the truth.

You learned the *Nevertheless Principle* in week four to help you get convinced. Let's revisit it now.

The Nevertheless Principle

When you need to reset your Heart Logic, turn a little "t" truth into a Big "T" Truth, or plant your heart in a Big "S" Strategy, you need one strategic word: nevertheless.

It becomes a transformative word when you let it bridge the gap between your experience or feeling and God's Big "T" Truth. You acknowledge what you lived, follow it with "nevertheless," and guide your heart into a more authentic reality.

Hebrews 4:12 (TPT) reminds us, "For we have the living Word of God, which is full of energy, like a two-mouthed sword. It will even penetrate to the very core of our being where soul and spirit, bone and marrow meet! It interprets and reveals the true thoughts and secret motives of our hearts."

This means that although our experience was real, what God says (Big "T" Truths) can be trusted to transform our experience and bridge the gap into the unhindered life we desire to live with Him.

Although you have read a lot of scripture throughout this journey, there might be some impactful verses that quickly come to mind when thinking through your Big "T" Truths or maybe there are scriptures that are waiting just for your heart. God's Word is living and active.

Phase Four: *Fighting the Battle in Moments of Collision*
As you know so well by now, you have moments of collision ahead of you where your new normal collides with your old normal. These will be moments you feel triggered and enticed back to your old ways, and you'll have to choose which way you'll go. You've got to be armed and ready for those moments, anticipating them and equipped with powerful Big "T" Truth to guide you forward.

In week five, you were given three steps to follow when you face collisions.

1) *Stop*
2) *Think*
3) *Pray*

> *Take control of your heart, and unhindered life will find you.*

Second Corinthians 10:5 directs us, "We demolish arguments and every pretension that sets itself up against the knowledge of God, and we take captive every thought to make it obedient to Christ." We have three steps to follow to exercise that direction.

Stop. Interrupt yourself from leaning into the allure of the familiar in a moment of collision. Say "no" to the old normal full of little "t" truths and small "s" strategies.

Think. Let God remind you of the Big "T" Truths he's given you to quiet a triggered Sore Spot. Remember how personal they are and how there's no way you're the exception to Big "T" Truth. Say "yes" to your new normal and live out your Big "S" Strategies.

Pray. Invite God into that moment of collision with you. This isn't a cognitive battle. This is a spiritual battle. You need Him in it with you.

In order to Stop, Think, and Pray effectively, you can't scramble in the moment. You need to rehearse and know exactly what to remember.

It might sound like a shortened version of your *Nevertheless Statement:* "*I've been chosen by God, even when others aren't choosing me.*" "*God is with me, so risk isn't the enemy.*" "*You never have to prove yourself with God, so relax!*"

These are meant to hit your unique Sore Spot right in the bullseye and call your heart right back to the security it's longing for. Always remember, your heart has to be convinced that this statement is actually true before it's going to make any difference in your moments of collision. (See Appendix I for examples)

Phase Five: *Fighting the Battle by Protecting your Heart*
As you saw in week five, your journey of growth and healing lasts long after "aha" moments and initial healing encounters. Your journey won't sustain if you don't guard and protect those moments and encounters well. That is not because they aren't real. It's because you'll get fooled by your old normal again. The little "t" truths and small "s" strategies will convince you again that they're safer, easier, better, and you'll listen!

As you now know, you have to intentionally remember and rehearse what God has taught you. You also have to build a life that supports the new way of living you're building.

Let's review the *Remembrance Statement* you learned in week five that can be used as a tool to keep your heart planted on your new Big "T" Truths and Big "S" Strategies.

Remembrance Statement:

This statement comes from asking God, "What do you want me to remember about what is true (Big "T" Truths) and how you've called me to live (Big "S" Strategies)?" It will capture the heart of who you wanted to become when you first began this unhindered journey.

Let it reflect the Big "T" Truths that will shape how you see yourself, God, others, and the world. Let it reflect the Big "S" Strategies that show what it looks like for your genius to come alive and for you to perhaps love a little more selflessly, forgive a little quicker, or speak a little louder. (See Appendix H for examples)

These statements are meant to remind you of your new normal. As you rehearse this Remembrance Statement (daily in the beginning), you have the chance to get your heart more convinced of it each time you speak it. You also set your intention in the right direction every day, especially if you start your day with this. Lastly, you protect the gains you've already made by not letting them slip awareness or letting doubt creep in unnoticed. If you find resistance to believing your Remembrance Statement one day, it tells you that you've got some work to do. Explore the resistance. Maybe there's been a collision, and you need to reset. Maybe there's another layer of healing you need to do. Maybe you need to get the enemy off your back through prayer.

You Are Ready!

Stand confident at each phase of the growth and healing process. You can do this. Grab hold of these tools that are simple expressions of the lifelines God has offered us to let Him become our ultimate Heart Shaper! Wield them wisely. Wield them often. Take control of your heart, and unhindered life will find you.

What a celebration we've had this week! Unhindered life waits for us all! It's within our reach when we follow the pathway for healing and growth that guides our hearts into a new normal—a place where we live counterintuitively and therefore freely. We're equipped and ready with tools to lead us through this process and to guard us from falling back.

Will you take the invitation to move toward an unhindered life? Remember, unhindered living isn't perfect. But it's full of peace that comes through eternal hope and beauty even when we can't see hope and beauty on this earth. Unhindered living is not stagnant. It's ever increasing its reflection of Jesus. Unhindered living isn't living on the sidelines. It's living fully engaged in life and in relationships with eyes wide open to see those around you who need your help or love. Do you want that?

I hope you'll choose to unhinder your heart so you can live well, lead well, and finish well.

> Remember, unhindered living isn't perfect. But it's full of peace that comes through eternal hope and beauty even when we can't see hope and beauty on this earth.

Prayer:

God, your truth is power. Your love is freedom. Your presence is healing. Thank you that your Word is active and alive and can change me. It's not just for our heads to know but for our hearts to experience. As I lean into the tools you give me to unhinder my life, please strengthen my heart's resolve each time. May your Word and my awareness of your presence never leave me, and may I never forget the power of your love, mercy, and care to change me.

God, you are so good to me. I will praise you every day for the unending gifts you give when we follow your voice and your ways. I choose to pursue an unhindered life with you. Thank you for showing me that it's possible! Amen.

Reflection Questions:

Which tool will you need most for the phase of growth and healing you are in?

How can you prepare yourself to use this tool well? What preparation do you need? Do you need to get an environment ready for it? Do you need to get some courage or make this a priority in your life?

Dream about the unhindered life waiting for you. What are you looking forward to the most?

What stood out to you most in today's reading?

We have tools to look back, be present, and move forward in our unhindered journey!

WEEK 6: GROUP QUESTIONS

Use what you've written on the "TUL Pathway" diagram (See Appendix J) to tell the story of your heart.

If you have extra time, you can share answers to the questions below:

Share what has impacted you the most from doing the work in *Unhindered: Thirty Days*.

What are you looking forward to the most in your unhindered life?

How is God personally calling you to be a difference maker?

THE HINDERED HEART

A story written by flawed authors, compromising your ability to live freely and lightly. Living in a hindered narrative stalls your heart's emotional and spiritual development, producing a misaligned heart that revolves around yourself and your own life experiences.

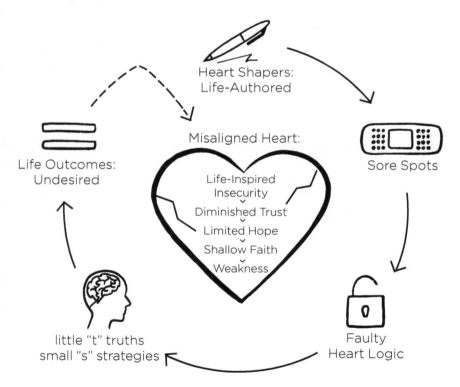

Heart Shapers:
Life-Authored

Misaligned Heart:

Life Outcomes:
Undesired

Sore Spots

Life-Inspired
Insecurity
˅
Diminished Trust
˅
Limited Hope
˅
Shallow Faith
˅
Weakness

little "t" truths
small "s" strategies

Faulty
Heart Logic

Heart Shapers: Life-Authored
The multidimensional influences that mold the shape of our hearts. Negative influences and impacts leave a mark on our hearts that doesn't align with God's design for us.

Sore Spots
The bruising or site of a wound in our hearts left by a negative Heart Shaper that becomes a filter within us, shaping (often unknowingly) our feelings, perceptions, and actions.

Faulty Heart Logic
Our heart answers "no" or makes exceptions about the goodness of God, ourselves, others, and/or life. Those answers set a faulty foundation for our more detailed thinking and doing in life.

little "t" truths
Our experiential truth that appears true because we've seen it, lived it, or felt it.

small "s" strategies
The things we do in order to try to be okay or feel protected, given the distorted reality that a little "t" truth has created.

Life Outcomes: Undesired
The undesired impacts on our lives (emotional, relational, spiritual, behavioral, physical, character) that result from the contents of our hearts being misaligned.

Misaligned Heart
A hindered heart that is insecure, unable to trust and hope, move forward in faith, and have strength to overcome, endure, and love.

THE UNHINDERED HEART

A story edited by God, giving us the ability to live freely and lightly. Becoming unhindered matures our hearts' emotional and spiritual development, producing aligned hearts that revolve around God's healing, freedom, and power in each piece of our stories.

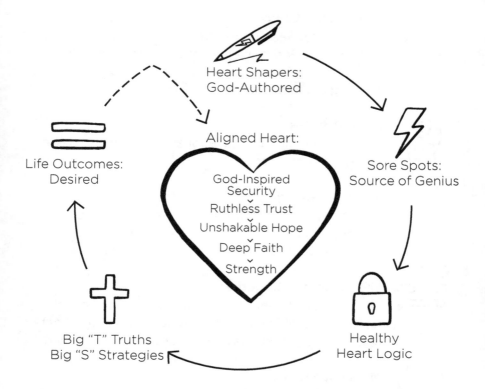

Heart Shapers:
God-Authored

Aligned Heart:

Life Outcomes:
Desired

God-Inspired
Security
⌄
Ruthless Trust
⌄
Unshakable Hope
⌄
Deep Faith
⌄
Strength

Sore Spots:
Source of Genius

Big "T" Truths
Big "S" Strategies

Healthy
Heart Logic

Heart Shapers: God-Authored

When the multidimensional influences that have molded the shape of our hearts, in the past, no longer have power because God's influence and authorship have taken their place.

Sore Spots: Source of Genius

The very best of us that shows up when a Sore Spot is healed by God and turned into purpose.

Healthy Heart Logic

Our heart answers "yes" about the goodness of God, ourselves, others, and life. Those answers set the healthy foundation for our more detailed thinking and doing in life.

Big "T" Truths

God's perspectives and realities (Truth) that lead us into health and abundance.

Big "S" Strategies

The postures and actions God intended for us that lead us into health and abundance.

Life Outcomes: Desired

The desired impacts on our lives (emotional, relational, spiritual, behavioral, physical, character) that result from the contents of our hearts being aligned with God.

Aligned Heart

An unhindered heart that is secure, able to trust and hope, move forward in faith, and has strength to overcome, endure, and love.

APPENDIX A:
HEART SHAPER TIMELINE

Note below the key moments, influences, events, or experiences from each period of your life. Try to include things that were both positive and negative. Use the list of Heart Shapers (with examples) to help guide your reflection.

Childhood:

Adolescence:

Early Adulthood:

Middle Adulthood:

Late Adulthood:

Look over the events and note:
The positive events/people that shaped your life.
The painful events/difficult people that have shaped your life.

After spending some time reviewing your list, highlight the 5 most impactful events/influences that you believe have been your most powerful, negative Heart Shapers. (Remember, they can be influential even if they are not dramatic or traumatic.) Some of your painful events/influences may also group together according to a common theme to create one Heart Shaper.

List your top five Heart Shapers below.

1)

2)

3)

4)

5)

Primary Heart Shapers:

1) *Biology.* Defined by your nature, personality, physical characteristics, and DNA.

   Negative examples: a disability that impacts your experience and identity, a predisposition to depression or anxiety, a driven nature

2) *Family.* The lessons, patterns, and impacts derived from a
   family of origin that have long-term effects.

   Negative examples: sibling rivalry, absent parent, explosive anger in the home, harsh or inconsistent family rules,
   abuse, abandonment, critical environment

3) *Everyday life experiences.* Moments that may not stand out
   individually but accumulate into messages that matter shape
   our hearts.

   Negative examples: a relationship ending, losing a job, disengaged spouse, repeated criticism, unattainable expectations, enduring a narcissist

4) *Defining Moments.* These are individual events that have
   an extremely strong impact for good or for bad. These can
   include "God moments" and mountaintop experiences as well
   as traumatic events.

   Negative examples: abuse, divorce, infidelity, death, major
   illness, significant loss

5) *Sin/Evil.* Your sin, others' sin, and spiritual warfare continue to
   shape your heart as you face circumstances, make decisions,
   and experience daily life.

   Negative examples: giving in to temptations, moral failures, sinful thoughts, impact from the sins of others

Secondary Heart Shapers:

6) *The Mind.* The way you think, understand, process, and perceive the world around you.

   Negative examples: black and white (all or nothing) thinking, rigid thinking, biased thinking

7) *Beliefs.* Your spiritual convictions, guiding principles, moral compass, and anchor points.

   Negative examples: unbiblical theology, immoral standards

8) *The Emerging Self-Concept.* What you learn about who you are, how you see yourself, an emerging self-concept.

   Negative examples: deciding "I'm stupid" after failure, concluding "No one wants me" after a rejection, judging "I'm defective" after a continued struggle

9) *Emotions.* Feelings and passions, the affective side of us, how our feelings attach meaning to life.

   Negative examples: being dominated by emotions, the influence of stuffed or unexamined emotions, the overwhelming state of emotions that leads to meaning making

10) *The Will.* Volition, desires, motivation for choices, the cognitive side of us that attaches meaning to circumstances and relationships.

   Negative examples: Insatiable will toward something—"I'll get whatever outcome I desire no matter the cost." "I'm always confused, but I must have an answer and a plan." "I know better than anyone—including God—how my life ought to go, and I'll make it happen."

APPENDIX B: SORE SPOTS

Examples of Sore Spots:

- Insecurity
- Inadequacy
- Shame
- Fear
- Rejection
- Pride
- Unvalued
- Abandoned
- Unimportant
- Unworthy

Connect your Heart Shapers to your Sore Spots. You may have the same Sore Spot connected to more than one Heart Shaper.

5 Primary Heart Shapers	Sore Spots
1)	1)
2)	2)
3)	3)
4)	4)
5)	5)

APPENDIX C:
little "t" truths and small "s" strategies

Examples of little "t" truths:

"It's weak to struggle."

"God needs me to contribute, so I can't slow down."

"Good leadership means always being in control."

"God takes too long to get things done, so I'll just help Him out."

"Feeling good about myself depends on how successful I am."

"Everything will be better if I just don't feel anything."

"Other people will just disappoint me."

"No one can handle the real you."

"I don't have anything to contribute."

"No one's intentions can be that good. People are always out for themselves."

Examples of small "s" strategies:

Hide: Be invisible or wear a mask.

- "Don't stand out."
- "Don't make waves."
- "Don't have opinions."
- "Keep up the right image."
- "Keep secrets and cover up."

Deny: Pretend nothing is wrong.

- "Just forget about it, and move on."
- "Put on a happy face."
- "Problem? What problem?"
- "Minimize your feelings and the situation."
- "Accept the fact that it's hopeless to look for real solutions."

Settle: Accept that this is as good as it gets.

- "Settle for mediocrity."

- "Accept the fact that nothing will ever get better."
- "Give up on yourself, someone else, or the situation."
- "Lower your standards."
- "Force yourself to be okay with things that just aren't okay."

Self-sufficiency: Over-rely on yourself.

- "Depend on yourself, be over-prepared, and always have a plan."
- "Always defend yourself."
- "Keep risk low by staying in charge."
- "Don't count on anyone for anything."
- "Put your walls up with others and protect yourself."
- "Don't let other people get to you."

Go numb: Don't risk feeling the weight of reality.

- "Don't feel anything. Protect yourself from hurt, pain, and heartache."
- "Shut off your emotions and become overly logical. Live in your head."
- "Don't pay attention to any emotions inside."
- "Above all, don't be vulnerable."
- "Wear a mask."

Compartmentalize: Separate parts of your life or identity to deal with incongruence.

- "Create different boxes inside of you to store incongruent information. Do this well and you can be okay with some pretty horrible things."
- "Separate your public and private life so you can keep secrets."
- "Separate your hurtful behavior from the rest of your identity. Give other people the same out."

Achieve: Keep performing and winning to try to feel valuable.

- "Always succeed. Always beat expectations. Always do better than anyone else."
- "Seek external validation to cover up the internal void."
- "Keep achieving to keep the praise coming."
- "Work harder to try to feel more valuable."

- "Be a perfectionist. Never settle for mere excellence."
- "Make sure to win when you play the comparison game."

Control: Keep everything under your influence.

- "Be in control of everything to shape the outcomes the way you think is best."
- "Dominate and overpower others."
- "Be three steps ahead of everyone else so you can outmaneuver them."
- "Always have a plan and manipulate your way into making it happen."
- "Force the outcomes you want when it doesn't look like they'll go your way."
- "Don't be vulnerable. Never depend on others."
- "Run away or check out when it looks like you won't get the outcome you want."
- "Always blame somebody else for mistakes or problems."
- "Read people really well so you can change your words and behavior to please them."

Stay busy: Cover things up with activity.

- "Fill your life with constant activities so you don't have to face what's inside you."
- "Don't slow down."
- "Take pride in being over-scheduled."
- "Value doing over being."
- "Ignore boundaries that protect personal time."

Indulge: Quiet the discomfort with unhealthy ways of soothing.

- "Self-medicate to feel better."
- "Over-value short term relief, and ignore the fact that it leads to long-term problems."
- "Drink too much; take pills you don't need; use drugs."
- "Over-indulge in a hobby or a mindless activity."
- "Cover up the problem with something that numbs you out."
- "Self-soothe in a destructive way that keeps the problem from being addressed."
- "Ignore consequences."

APPENDIX D: BIG "T" TRUTH

Here are some little "t" truths transformed into Big "T" Truths.

Healed Sore Spot: Righteousness
Examples of Big "T" Truths:

1) Grace is strong enough to overcome my worst moments because Christ died for me. (Ephesians 2:8)
2) God delights in me, even in my weaknesses and imperfections. (Zephaniah 3:17, Psalm 103:12)
3) Even my worst behavior doesn't define me because I'm a new creation in Christ. (2 Corinthians 5:17)

Healed Sore Spot: Safety
Big "T" Truths:

1) I can take God-orchestrated risks because God is trustworthy. (Psalm 9:10, Joshua 1:9)
2) Bad things can happen, but God is sovereign over them all and uses them for my good and His glory. (Isaiah 46:10, Romans 8:28)
3) Following God's will and letting Him be in control means that I don't always have to anticipate and prepare for everything that might happen. (Proverbs 3:5-6)

Healed Sore Spot: God-Given Esteem
Big "T" Truths:

1) I don't need to have all the talents or intelligence because the Holy Spirit lives in me, making me better than I am. (2 Corinthians 12:9)
2) I'm a citizen of heaven. God has given me the tools to be the salt and light of the world. (Philippians 3:20, Matthew 5:13-14)
3) My value isn't dependent on my performance; my performance is simply my service. (Ephesians 2:8-9, Romans 11:6)

Healed Sore Spot: Significance

Big "T" Truths:

1) I'm united with God, and I belong in His family."(1 Corinthians 6:17, 1 Corinthians 12:27)
2) I've been bought with a price, which shows how much God values me. (1 Corinthians 6:19-20)
3) I've been chosen and given a purpose. God delights in me. (1 Peter 2:9-10, John 15:16, Psalm 147:11, Zephaniah 3:17)

Healed Sore Spot: Cherished

Big "T" Truths:

1) God pursues me relentlessly and wants to be with me. (Psalm 139:7-8, Matthew 18:12, James 4:8)
2) God calls me precious and cares about every detail of my life. (Proverbs 3:15, Ephesians 2:10, Matthew 6:26)
3) God sees me and knows me intimately. (Psalm 139:13, Genesis 16:13, Hebrews 4:13)

Healed Sore Spot: Humility

Big "T" Truths:

1) God knows all, but I don't. He is the author of life, and I can submit with joy because I'm sure He knows far better than me. (Psalm 97:9, Revelation 22:13)
2) I'm called to think of others more than myself and humble myself before them. (Philippians 2:3, Romans 12:16, Ephesians 4:2)
3) God rejoices when I lay down my needs and desires for the sake of another. (John 15:13, James 4:6, Luke 14:11)

APPENDIX E: BIG "S" STRATEGIES

Examples of Big "S" Strategies:

1) *Live vulnerably: Hold your head high and live openly and authentically in relationships with people you trust.* (James 5:16, Galatians 6:2, 2 Timothy 2:15)
   - Let yourself be seen and known.
   - Use your voice.
   - Confess secrets and bring dark to light.

2) *Face reality: Lean into "grace plus truth" to fully acknowledge your pain and struggles.* (John 1:14, Psalm 34:17-18, Psalm 55:22, 1 Peter 5:7)
   - Dissolve fear and shame with the wonder of God's grace—a grace that enables vulnerability.
   - Be real with yourself about the parts of you that aren't okay.
   - Let trusted others know when you're hurting and confused.

3) *Pursue discipleship: Go beyond what's easy and known, and chase after God's purposes.* (Hebrews 6:1, Hebrews 5:12-14, Luke 17:5, Isaiah 48:10)
   - Strive for greater emotional and spiritual health.
   - Match your standards with God's standards.
   - Initiate change and keep pursuing something more.
   - Dream God-sized dreams.

4) *Depend: Be more God-reliant than self-reliant, and lean on trusted others.* (Proverbs 3:5, Psalm 62:5-6, Proverbs 27:17, Galatians 6:2)
   - Trust God to show you how.

- Embrace your weaknesses as opportunities for God's glory to be displayed.
- Let others help you.
- Trust others when they show themselves to be trustworthy.

5) *Acknowledge and manage your feelings: Experience life to the full.* (John 10:10, Ecclesiastes 3:4, Romans 12:15, John 11:35)
   - Acknowledge and embrace your feelings so God can use them to show you the assumptions, right or wrong, underneath them.
   - Don't fear emotions. Be confident that God will help you manage them.
   - Consider your emotions along with logic as you assess, decide, and conclude.
   - Be real with those you trust about what's in your heart.

6) *Integrate: Assimilate all parts of your life into your awareness, identity, and self-image.* (Proverbs 11:3, 1 John 1:9)
   - Be honest with yourself.
   - Pay attention to your internal nudges.
   - Develop "psychological distance" so you can observe how you feel, think, and act. Make any needed corrections.
   - Take your mask off and let people see the real you, trusting who you are in Christ.

7) *Simply serve: Rest in your God-given esteem so you can achieve as part of your service, not as a pursuit of personal success.* (Colossians 3:23-24, John 7:24, Hebrews 11:6)
   - Rest in the security of who you are apart from your performance. Embrace your God-given value.
   - Let God's smile mean more than the praise of others.
   - Celebrate when you've done well. Be satisfied and content with the good.
   - Measure success by how faithful you've been, not how much you've produced.

8) *Partner with God: Let God be your leader, trusting that He is capable and good.* (John 15:5, Colossians 1:17, 1 Chronicles 29:11-12, Jeremiah 10:23, Isaiah 30:21)
   - Don't run ahead of God. Submit and surrender to His leading and promptings.
   - Remember your partnership. Do your part and let God do His.
   - Relax and accept the outcomes God has for you, knowing He is always good.
   - Be flexible and adaptable.

9) *Abide: Slow down enough to be fully present in all situations.* (Matthew 6:34, John 15:10, Psalm 16:11)
   - Live with enough margin to allow you to put aside the undone and focus on the present moment.
   - Create moments of stillness to hear God's whispers.
   - Value being with God as well as doing things for Him.
   - Let God show you the right things to say "yes" to.

10) *Heal: Let God heal the pain you've tried to cover up so you can be your true self.* (2 Timothy 1:7, Psalm 34:18, 2 Kings 20:5)
   - Stop masking the pain and let God be your healer.
   - Replace the quick fix for the ultimate healing.
   - Let God's presence in your pain be your source of comfort.
   - Develop a plan to manage impulses and temptations, and submit them to God.

APPENDIX F:
LIFE OUTCOMES

Examples of Unhealthy Life Outcomes:

Emotional:
> Self-condemnation, Depression, Anxiety, Lack of fulfillment, On edge, Anger

Relational:
> Overly dependent on others, Bring out the worst in others, Hold onto resentments, Unproductive conflict, Lack of intimacy

Spiritual:
> Distance from God, Spiritual dryness, Self-sufficiency, Lack of surrender, Anger with God

Behavioral:
> Selfish choices, Self-indulgence, Self-medicating, Living with no margin, Paralyzed decision making, Lashing out

Physical:
> Lack of self-care, Unhealthy physical body

Character:
> Deceitful, Self-inflation, Rigidity, Impatient, Undependable, Dominating

Examples of Healthy Life Outcomes:

Emotional:
> Self-acceptance, Peace, Calm, Contentment, Secure, Joy

Relational:
> Healthy dependency on others, Bring out the best in others, Grace for others, Healthy interpersonal conflict

Spiritual:
> Intimacy with God, Partnership with God, Surrendered and submitted to God as your leader

Behavioral:
   Serve others, Self-control, Healthy self-sacrifice, Healthy rhythms, Take healthy risks

Physical:
   Healthy self-care, Healthy physical body

Character:
   Integrity, Humble, Accept limits, Flexible, Patient, Faithful

APPENDIX G: NEVERTHELESS STATEMENTS

Examples of Nevertheless Statements:

"God didn't bring justice the way I wanted Him to; nevertheless, God cares about this more than I do." (Isaiah 46:4, Psalm 46:10, Psalm 32:8)

"I have messed up so badly and I feel like a screw-up; nevertheless, I'm still valued because of God's sufficient grace." (2 Corinthians 12:9, 2 Corinthians 12:10, 2 Corinthians 3:5)

"My trust was broken multiple times by people I trusted; nevertheless, God will never fail me." (Joshua 21:45, Deuteronomy 7:9)

"Life has been incredibly hard; nevertheless, God is with me in my sorrow and creates purpose in the pain." (John 16:33, John 3:16, Psalm 23:4, Romans 5:2-5)

"I was abused for years; nevertheless, God rescued me from it. In fact, He was in the middle of it with me the whole time, urging me to feel His loving presence." (Psalm 16:11, Psalm 23:4)

APPENDIX H: REMEMBRANCE STATEMENTS

Examples of Remembrance Statements:

Personal Declaration:

> *I'm valuable; I'm good enough (Ephesians 1:7, Psalm 139:14). I don't have to be someone I'm not. I don't have to be just like my mom or my dad or anyone else because I'm God's creation— my shyness, the struggle with alcohol, and my strengths, too (Ephesians 3:12). I don't have to impress everyone and keep them happy. I just have to please God, and it's easy to make Him smile (Zephaniah 3:17, 1 John 4:8, Mark 12:30-32). With a repentant heart, I'm cleansed from all unrighteousness (1 John 1:9). He has turned my crimson sins white as snow (Isaiah 1:18). Therefore, I'll be bold and use my voice to speak into the hearts of God's people, according to His unique purposes for me (2 Corinthians 3:12, Joshua 1:9, Jeremiah 29:11). I will step out of the shadow of my parents and their legacy (where I've always felt the safest) and join God to continually discover ways He wants me to serve. I won't hold back because I remember that the Holy Spirit lives in me, and I can rely on His strength and wisdom as I join God on the mission He's given me (Jeremiah 1:9, Isaiah 61:1-2).*

Letter from God:

Dear John,

You don't have to worry (Philippians 4:6: *"Do not be anxious about anything, but in everything, by prayer and petition, with thanksgiving, present your request to God."*) **about looking stupid or being humiliated. You don't have to worry about your lack of strength. Stand in the strength of My might and not your own.** (Isaiah 40:31: *"But those who hope in the Lord will renew their strength. They will soar on wings like eagles; they will run and not grow weary, they will walk and not be faint."*) (Psalm 46:1: *"God is our refuge and strength, an ever-present help in trouble."*) (1 Peter 4:11: *"If anyone speaks, he should do it as one speaking the very words of God. If anyone serves, he should do it with the strength God provides, so that in all things God may be praised through Jesus Christ. To him be the glory and power forever and ever. Amen."*)

I have called you by name, John, (Isaiah 43:1: *"But now, this is what the Lord says—he who created you, O Jacob, he who formed you O Israel: 'Fear not, for I have redeemed you; I have called you by name; you are mine."*) **and asked you to join with Me in battling for the hearts of Christian leaders.** (Revelation 2:17: *"He who has an ear, let him hear what the Spirit says to the churches. To him who overcomes, I will give some of the hidden manna. I will also give him a white stone with a new name written on it, known only to him who receives it."*)

Trust Me (Proverbs 3:5-6: *"Trust in the Lord with all your heart and lean not on your own understanding; in all your ways acknowledge him, and he will make your paths straight."*) **and not your preparation or competency. Live a life of faith** (Hebrews 11:6: *"And without faith it is impossible to please God, because anyone who comes to him must believe that he exists* *and that he rewards those who earnestly seek him.")* **not fear.** *(2 Timothy 1:7: "For God did not give us a spirit of timidity, but a spirit of power, of love and of self-discipline, or a sound mind.")*

Depend on Me, not yourself. *(John 15:1-5: "I am the true vine and my Father is the gardener. He cuts off every branch in me that bears no fruit, while every branch that does bear fruit he trims clean so that it will be even more fruitful. You are already clean because of the word I have spoken to you. Remain in me and I will remain in you. No branch can bear fruit by itself; it must remain in the vine. Neither can you bear fruit unless you remain in me. I am the vine and you are the branches. If a man remains in me and I in him, he will bear much fruit; apart from me you can do nothing.")*

Be holy in word and deed. *(1 Peter 1:15-16: "But just as he who called you is holy, so be holy in all you do, for it is written, be holy for I am holy.")* **Humble yourself before Me and others.** *(Isaiah 66:2b: "This is the one I esteem: he who is humble and contrite and trembles at my word.")* *(Ephesians 4:2-3: "Be completely humble and gentle, be patient bearing with one another in love. Make every effort to keep the unity of the Spirit through the bond of peace.")* *(James 4:10: "Humble yourselves before the Lord, and he will lift you up.")*

John, above all, be strong and of good courage as you face different challenges in your life. Don't be disheartened or dismayed, even when you are in over your head, for have not I, the Lord your God, promised that I will be with you wherever you go? *(Joshua 1:9: "Have I not commanded you? Be strong and courageous. Do not be afraid; do not be discouraged, for the LORD your God will be with you wherever you go.")*

Your Abba

APPENDIX I: BATTLE-READY STATEMENTS FOR STOP, THINK, PRAY

Examples of Battle-Ready Statements for Stop, Think, Pray:

- I don't let fear get ahead of my faith.
- I am enough even when other people don't show it.
- When I feel ignored, God still sees me and knows me.
- I can trust God with any outcome.
- I am bold because the Spirit lives in me.
- It only matters what God thinks.
- I have been given a spirit of power, love, and self-discipline (2 Timothy 1:7).
- Speak up! My voice matters.
- When God's in it, risk isn't stupid.
- I am not defined by my sin. Grace is bigger.

APPENDIX J: WRITING THE STORY OF YOUR HEART

It's important that you learn to tell the whole story of your heart and see it as one cohesive and integrated story, not several disjointed parts. Take some time to write out each piece of your heart's story that you've learned along the way.

The Unhindered Life Pathway

Heart Shapers:

1)

2)

3)

4)

5)

Sore Spots:

1)

2)

3)

4)

5)

Heart Logic:

1)

2)

3)

4)

5)

little "t" truths:

1)

2)

3)

4)

5)

small "s" strategies:

1)

2)

3)

4)

5)

Life Outcomes:

1)

2)

3)

4)

5)

BIG "T" TRUTHS:

1)

2)

3)

4)

5)

BIG "S" STRATEGIES:

1)

2)

3)

4)

5)

LIFE OUTCOMES:

1)

2)

3)

4)

5)

NEVERTHELESS STATEMENTS:

PERSONAL DECLARATION:

LETTER FROM GOD:

CPSIA information can be obtained
at www.ICGtesting.com
Printed in the USA
BVHW070506161222
654335BV00015B/1152